D0407127

500
TERRIFIC
IDEAS
FOR
Organizing
Everything

Sheree Bykofsky

GALAHAD BOOKS
NEW YORK

A Round Stone Press Book.

Directors: Marcia Melnick, Paul Fargis, Susan E. Meyer
Design: Jeff Fitschen
Illustrations: Ray Skibinski

First Galahad Books edition published in 1997.

Published by Galahad Books
A division of BBS Publishing Corporation
450 Raritan Center Parkway
Edison, NJ 08837

Galahad Books is a registered trademark of BBS Publishing Corporation.

Published by arrangement with Round Stone Press, Inc.

This is a special edition
distributed by Sterling Publishing Co., Inc.
387 Park Avenue South
New York, NY 10016

Library of Congress Catalog Number: 96-79815
ISBN: 1-57866-150-1
Printed in the United States of America.

Contents

Introduction

At home and away, at work, at school, and at play, being organized touches every aspect of your life. It means being prepared for meetings or shopping trips; being neat and orderly in the way you present yourself and in the way you arrange your belongings; remembering appointments and ideas; being on time and allowing enough time for all you have to do. Being organized involves keeping track of a wide variety of things; it means keeping track of people, updating address lists, and remembering birthdays and other occasions; and it means keeping track of your thoughts so you can make clear arguments orally and in writing. In short, it means developing the tools for living a happy, productive life.

This book provides both general organizing principles and specific applications. To avoid confusion, I chose not to include a lot of cross-references, instead assigning ideas to their most logical or useful category. For example, specific kitchen storage ideas can be found under the "Kitchen" heading, whereas general storage techniques, which you can apply to your kitchen if you wish, can be found under "Storage."

An important part of being organized is finding just the right product to suit your needs. I've included product information wherever I thought it would be helpful. If you can't find a product mentioned in this book, dial information at 1-800-555-1212 and ask the operator for the toll-free number of the manufacturer. Or, if the company isn't listed, try the operator in the state where the company is located. You'll find that many manufacturers do not sell their products directly to consumers, but they'll be more than happy to point you in the direction of the dealer nearest you.

One last word of advice: Being organized is an ideal, a goal to move toward, not a state to achieve. To expect perfection in anything is to invite defeat. Use the ideas here to eliminate some of the clutter that slows you down and to streamline your routine procedures. Use them creatively and they will help you design your own organizing systems to bring order directly to the parts of your life that need it most.

Acknowledgements:

I could never have accumulated 500 terrific ideas without the kind and generous support of organized friends and colleagues. I am grateful, too, to Melissa Schwarz and Constance Jones, who expertly edited my manuscript into a book. Warm thanks to the following wonderful people who contributed or inspired ideas: Dianne Johansson-Adams; Christian and Lea Andrade; Don Aslett; Heidi Atlas; Alice Miller Bregman; Rosalind Bykofsky (my Mom); Kathy Clark; Larry Dark; Trisha Drain; Mia Ellison; Paul Fargis; Mary Flynn; Linda Gruber; Dian Hamilton; Tobi Haynes; Barbara Hemphill; Jann Jasper; Lois Kahan; Joyce Kaplan; Doris Latino; Ellen Massey; Marsha Melnick; Susan Meyer; Carol Mills; Elaine Martin Petrowski; Phillip Rafield; Adele Ribelow; Janet Rosen; Liz Sanchez; Jeannie Sass; Peggy Schmidt; Norman Schreiber; Derek Solomon; Michael and Aida Solomon; Susan Spieler; and Helen Stambler.

But I owe the most to Diane Roback and Ken Anderson. Five hundred, no five thousand, thanks to each of them, and five thousand kisses to my patient, supportive, organized husband, Steve Solomon.

A special thanks goes to the following companies for assisting me in my research: Rubbermaid, Casio, Rolodex, Symantec, Dome, Lion Office Products, and Anthes Universal.

I am also indebted to the following stores, companies, and corporations for their help: Abracadata, Barson Hardware, BC Office Products, Better Living Products, Binney & Smith, Borland, Budget Buddy, Clairson International, Class Act, ClassCase, Conimar, CSD, Currier & Seedboro, Day Runner, Day-Timer, DeBoer & Co, Dek, Delco Office Systems, Design Ideas, DRG Stationery, Duo-Tang, Elfa, Esselte Pendaflex, Filofax, First Marketing Ltd., Glacier Software, Helix USA, Heller, HiPro, Hitchcock Publications, Hold Everything Store, Kentex, Laundry Bags Unlimited, Lee/Rowan, Lifestyle Software Group, Microcomputer Accessories, OIA, Safco, Smith Metal Arts, Spectrum Diversified Design, The Stanley Works, Sterling, Velcro, Vertiflex, and Wirth International.

Note: None of the product manufacturers mentioned in this book paid to be included, nor was any company promised mention or endorsement. My product recommendations do not constitute endorsement.

ORGANIZING BASICS

1 think vertical

When organizing items for storage, packing, or filing, avoid putting them in piles. Things get buried in piles. Use hanging folders in your file drawers; vertical hot files on your desk and for sorting mail; and shelves and grids for storing things on walls or on the backs of closet doors.

2 workstations

Set up a central station for every routine task, be it mailing, preparing breakfast, paying bills, writing letters, or doing laundry. Design the station to suit the task. Keep all necessary tools within easy reach. Aim to create workstations that are easy to use, well equipped, attractive, and orderly.

3 be creative

Walk around your home. Are some items just taking up space or going to waste? Think of new uses for them. Use a straw basket as a planter, for example, or to display guest soap in your bathroom. Use a spare photo album for recipes or a stamp collection. Use a notebook as a travel diary. Use your imagination.

4 good riddance

Get in the habit of dating everything, or simply circle the dates on all your purchases. Then set aside a regular time to get rid of anything out of date that isn't collectible. This organizing principle applies not only to prescriptions and perishable food items, but to travel books, calendars, old restaurant and shopping guides, books containing lots of dated material, newspapers, and magazines.

5 get set

Keep sets together: clothing sets, teapot sets, games, sheets. Anything that requires another part to operate at its best should be stored with all its parts together (or very near each other).

6 get help

Sometimes you just can't do it all by yourself. Enlist a friend to help you with a project you've been avoiding. Perhaps you have a service you can offer in return. Or hire someone to do some of the work—a student or a professional, depending on the task and your budget.

7 they know best

If you can't figure out how to organize something, look for a model. In other words, to organize your books, adopt the system used by a library or bookstore; for ideas on how to organize your compact disks, visit a major music store. Tour an art supply store, a knitting store, and a stationery store for good ideas that can apply to other materials as well, and consider purchasing their specialized organizational equipment.

8 do the one-step

If you think you're too busy to spend time organizing, you actually have more incentive to be organized than someone who has all the time and energy in the world to make messes and "fix them later." Hang up your coat in the closet immediately when you come inside, rather than (1) throwing the coat on a chair; (2) throwing the coat on the floor so you can sit on the chair; (3) taking the coat to the cleaners because it has become dirty and rumpled from being tossed around on the floor, and then (4) hanging it up in the closet. The rule is: Take a little time to do it now, or take a lot of time to do it later.

9 your choice

It's easier to learn and retain good habits than to correct bad habits. Therefore, in everything you do, make a conscious effort to learn how to do it right before plunging in. As much as is practical, think through all processes and routines in advance. Read directions, talk to experts, and don't proceed until you feel ready.

10 map it out

Plan before you start. Whether you're working, shopping, or traveling, almost everything takes longer if you don't envision the big picture ahead of time. Planning also prevents foul-ups. You wouldn't set off on a long trip without a map. In life, as in driving, you need to have directions but to be flexible when you run into traffic and tie-ups.

11 my idea

In life, unlike in driving, you can often make the rules. Avoid following other people's complicated plans unless you thoroughly understand, and preferably agree with, the logic. Whenever possible, devise your own plan.

12 mental checklist

Before you go out, take a moment to visualize your trip and anticipate what you'll need—whether it is your deposit slip for the bank, your check-cashing card for the supermarket, your gym card and locker key for the gym, your map for a trip, or your money, credit cards, or checkbook for shopping.

13 a special charity

If you're reluctant to throw things out, especially things you feel sentimental about or things that might have some value to someone else, look for especially appropriate charities. For example, in *Conquering the*

Paper Pile-Up, author Stephanie Culp recommends donating old Christmas cards to a certain home for abused and abandoned children: St. Jude's Ranch for Children, Box 985, Boulder City, Nevada 89005. The children cut up your old cards, make new ones, and then sell them to finance their facility.

14 it's right over here

In general, things should be stored as close as possible to where you're most likely to use them. Keep your desk well-stocked with everyday supplies such as pens, paper, and stamps; keep your bathroom cleaning products in the bathroom; keep tablecloths in or near the kitchen or dining room; keep the television remote on or near the television.

15 this is the day

At home and at work, name one day a month "Organizing Day." Put it in your calendar and consider it an important appointment. Metaphorically and physically, clear some space for yourself. Note where you waste time, and make an effort to be more efficient. Take the time to put organizers in your drawers, throw out old files, donate books to the library, or add shelves to a closet.

16 watch out

Many organizing products help you save time, and streamline activities in your home and office, but avoid using so many organizers that you need to organize them! Sometimes simpler is better.

17 day by day

Being organized is an ongoing process. Make a vow to yourself to spend fifteen minutes every day completing one high-priority task, and keep at it until it's finished. If you do miss one day, make it up the next, but don't let important projects go. By putting in a little time every day you stay connected to the project and will probably find yourself motivated to finish it faster than you expected.

18 that's all she wrote

You should never have to search for a pen. Keep at least one in a designated place in every room of the house and in every pocketbook and notebook. If possible, keep a pad with the pen. For the kitchen, look for a magnetic pen that will stick to the refrigerator. If you're lucky, you can find one that's also a combination can opener and bottle opener.

19 alternate brain

Lists are basic to organization. Just like adding more RAM to your computer, think of making lists as a way of expanding your own memory capacity. As soon as you have a clever idea or think of something that needs to be done, either do it at once or write it down. Writing it down increases the chances that you will follow through and frees your mind to think of new things.

20 reorganize

Always reassess your routine, especially if it feels like a hindrance or productivity begins to lag. Flexibility is essential to good time management. In fact, it's safe to say that in organizing, as in life, change is the only constant.

21 no laws

Do whatever works for you. There's no rule saying that sheets must go in linen closets or that shirts can't be folded with shorts. If it makes sense for you, put kitchen towels and soaps in the kitchen cabinet. Use your address book for project ideas, your refrigerator for keeping nail polish, your ice bucket as a vase, and your ice cube trays as drawer organizers.

22 more than once

You may have heard the guilt-producing fallacy that you should handle any piece of paper only once. Most professional organizers today agree that this advice is nonsense. You may need to check a letter, bill, or advertisement more than once, but try to keep your paper handling to a minimum. Just make sure you are productive each time you handle a paper, even if you merely indicate where the paper is to be filed and throw it into a box marked "To be filed."

ACTIVITIES

23 not to be missed

Keep a folder of announcements of coming events that you may be interested in attending (sales, fairs, ballets, benefits, lectures, concerts, etc.). In addition, mark the events on your calendar in pencil or use a colored ink to differentiate them from actual appointments. Include an abbreviated notation on the calendar, such as "see folder," to remind yourself to check the announcement for details. Keep your announcement folder with other active folders. Purge the file regularly, and don't try to do everything!

24 tickets

When you buy tickets in advance for an event such as a ball game, ballet, or concert, keep the tickets in your wallet or in a place where you will see them often, such as tacked to a bulletin board. Mark the event in your appointment book or on your calendar, and if there's a chance of forgetting, add a note to yourself: "Take tickets."

25 packed with organization

If you use the gym a lot, you may want to invest in a

locker bag. They're typically rectangular in shape, come in a variety of materials, and are equipped with many special features. All have lots of pockets and zippers for holding and separating clean laundry, dirty laundry, wet swimsuits, valuables, papers, razors, refillable water bottles, and toiletries. The best feature is a separate ventilated compartment for sneakers. Locker bags fit in most lockers as well as under standard airplane seats and in overhead compartments. Some have racquet holders, removable shoulder straps, and specialized gear holders. Find the one that best suits your needs and budget.

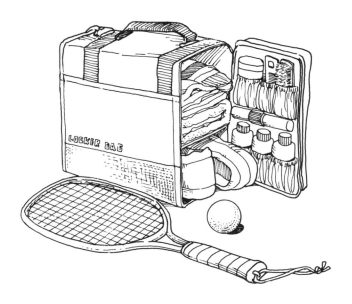

26 knit to fit

If your knitting needles and yarns are bursting out of a plastic shopping bag, do yourself a favor and go to a knitting store. Chances are they have just the bag or storage box you need. If they don't, think about making your next knitting project a knitting bag. Sew lots of pockets inside to hold needles and other equipment.

27 speaking of knitting

Has it been fifteen years since you picked up your knitting needles? Was your half-made baby bunting intended for someone who's in college now? Is your valuable storage space filled with half-built model airplanes or unused art supplies? Face it, you've moved on. Find a child with an interest in your lost craft or hobby, or give your unfinished project to a charity, but don't let it clutter your home.

28 extra drawer space?

Instead of using a bag for your knitting, sewing, model airplane kits, or other craft, consider creating a hobby drawer. Add drawer organizers to separate each element of the hobby, and use a desk, countertop, or bureau as work space. If your hobby requires lots of space or if you have lots of hobbies, create a hobby center around a desk or chest of drawers.

29 multiple CDs

If your CD player holds multiple compact disks, keep the empty containers stacked in order while they're playing so you'll know what you're listening to and can put the CDs away easily when you're finished. The same goes for records.

30 VCRelief

The VCR is the best time organizer ever invented for TV watchers because it allows you to watch on your own schedule. Take advantage of the flexibility. Keep lots of blank tapes on hand. If you're watching TV and the phone rings, you can start taping and see what you missed later. If you're viewing a tape, remember that you can stop it to do something else and continue watching when you're done.

31 zap 'em

VCRs really cut down on the amount of time it takes to watch a show. You can watch most half-hour shows in about fifteen or twenty minutes if you fast-forward through the commercials. Game shows go even faster if you zap not only the commercials but the slow contestants who spend light-years contemplating puzzles you solved in a minute.

32 what's on tonight?

If you have a VCR that allows you to tape several programs in a row by using a timer, try this system to organize your taping. Load a blank tape into your VCR. Sit down with your program guide and make a list on a large Post-it of the shows you plan to tape. Program the tape. As long as that tape is in the VCR, keep the list on top of the TV. That way, you'll know what's on the tape when you sit down to watch it. When the tape is full, remove it and attach the list to the tape. Insert a new blank tape in the VCR, and start a new list.

33 station identification

If you have cable TV, you'll know what I'm talking about. There are so many stations, and the stations listed do not correspond to the channels on your set! Don't throw down your remote in anger. Request a list of what's what from the cable station company and tape it to the side of your TV (using Tacky Tape on the back so that the tape doesn't show). If your cable company won't cooperate, spend an hour one night watching each station until it identifies itself. Then type your own list.

34 movie madness

Say good-bye to those old 8-millimeter and super-8 three-minute movie reels that burn when you try to show them on your rickety old movie projector. Transfer all your old films to videotape. Many photo developers offer this service; check the yellow pages to find one that does. If you're too sentimental to get rid of the movie reels, you can keep them—just store them neatly.

35 decide once

Read the television program guide with a highlighting pen and highlight your choices. If you like, use a second color to highlight your alternate choices and a third color to indicate programs you intend to tape. Highlighting saves you from having to reread the guide time after time.

36 home entertainment centers

When deciding what kind of home entertainment unit to build or buy, measure all your entertainment equipment, electronic components, and tapes, CDs, and records. Then measure the space. Leave as much room as possible to allow your collections to grow and to allow you to add components. Sliding shelves are a plus for reaching equipment stored to the rear. Sliding drawers hold lots of small items neatly. Remember, too, that electronic components have vents and need breathing room. Don't block the holes!

37 beach pack

During the months when you frequent the beach or pool, keep your beach bag packed with a hat or visor, towel, sunglasses, pen and paper, suntan lotion, umbrella, and a list of things to add at the last minute, such as a cooler, reading material, or headphones. This "keep-it-packed" principle can also be applied to gym bags, briefcases, luggage, baby bags, and so on.

ADDRESSES, PHONE NUMBERS, BUSINESS CARDS, & MESSAGES

38 safe at home

Never carry the only copy of your phone numbers. When you travel, compile a duplicate book or a smaller book of just those numbers you may need on the road.

39 if you have it, use it

If your phone has a memory, take the time to program frequently dialed numbers. This saves a lot of looking-up and dialing time!

40 Rolodex

It's not a coincidence that most organized businesspeople use a rolling card file called a Rolodex for storing their addresses and phone numbers. What you may not know is that Rolodex makes card files specifically designed for home and school as well as office use. Go to an office supply store, and have a look.

41 phone register

Many busy executives ask their secretaries to record messages in phone call registers, such as the Avery Phone Message Book. These make carbonless duplicates, triplicates, or even quadruplicates of every message, and there are usually several perforated message sheets per page. The top copy is for delivering the message and should be kept until the call is completed. The second copy stays in the book and provides a permanent record of everyone who has called. The record provides a backup source for phone numbers and a good starting point for creating a mailing list.

42 A is for appliance store

In your phone book, it's not always best to list numbers only by last name or even by company name. You run the risk of forgetting the location of infrequently used numbers, especially numbers for people who perform services for you on an irregular basis. So, at home or at work, regardless of whether you use a Rolodex, an address book, or a hand-held computer, think up easy-to-remember places for these numbers. Put the plumber under *P* and the carpenter under *C*. On occasion, you may want to crosslist these entries by name as well.

43 instant card

Keep a number of blank Rolodex cards after the *Z's* so you can find one quickly. It also saves time to staple a business card right onto a Rolodex card. If necessary, trim the top of the business card off to keep the Rolodex easy to flip through.

44 more than addresses

Don't use Rolodex cards only for names and numbers. On certain cards, include other information as well. For example, indicate time zones by noting, "One hour earlier," or "Six hours later." Use the back of the card as well for personal information or things you want to remember, such as who recommended the person to you or the project he or she worked on. Rolodex cards can also keep track of information that isn't related to a particular person, such as service agreement numbers, serial numbers, or credit card numbers. File these cards under logical headings, or file them alphabetically in a separate place at the back of your Rolodex.

45 marginal cards

When you receive a business card, wait before incorporating it into your permanent file. Instead, mark the date on the back, and some information about the person, and put it in a marginal box for six months. If you haven't used the card in that time, toss it.

46 clean out

Go through your Rolodex or telephone directory periodically and remove people whom you haven't called in a year, couldn't imagine ever calling, or don't remember. Dump 'em.

47 wallet pals

Make up a list of the names and phone numbers of the ten or twenty people you call most often. Reduce this list on a photocopy machine until it can be cut to the size of a credit card. Slip it into a clear credit-card holder, have it laminated at the photo store, or lay it over cardboard and cover it with clear plastic wrapping tape. Keep it in your wallet in a credit card slot. When necessary, update the list.

48 easy fix

If you keep addresses in an address book, use a pencil or erasable ink. That way you can erase entries when people move or change numbers. Erasing is much neater than crossing out, and it saves having to redo your address book.

49 make new friends but keep the old

Don't lose old friends and business contacts when they change their addresses or phone numbers. When you receive a change of address notice, enter the information into your permanent address book or Rolodex right away. If the person or business has not yet moved, set the notice aside and make a note on your calendar to transfer the information to your permanent records on the moving date.

50 that number again

List frequently called numbers on the first or last page of your address book or Rolodex: the phone company, the post office, the library, airline companies, bus and train information, and so on.

51 ready, set, mail

If you find yourself typing out mailing labels to the same people every day, take the time to organize the procedure. Either type out a bunch of labels to these people or, better yet, use your computer to preprint batches of labels ahead of time. Keep them alphabetically sorted in a small vertical file right near your mailing station.

APPOINTMENT BOOKS, CALENDARS, & PERSONAL DATA ORGANIZERS

52 first things first

The first entry in your appointment book should be: "If lost please return to : Name _____ Address _____ Phone _____." If blank spaces are provided for this information, fill them in. Something you carry with you every day is likely to be misplaced now and then, even if you're the most organized person in the world.

53 confirm

Whenever you make an appointment, jot down in your appointment book the telephone number of the person with whom you have made the appointment and agree to confirm your appointment that morning or the day before. Even if you haven't agreed to confirm, it's still a good idea. After all, the other person may not be as organized as you and may not have properly noted the time, date, or meeting place.

54 personal organization systems

Many creative and busy people have traded in their miscellaneous appointment books, address books, lists, credit card holders, and loose pens for a single personal organization planner that does it all—and more. Two of the most popular ones that are sold in stationery, gift, and office supply stores are Day Runner and Filofax. They come in a variety of sizes and can be customized to suit your individual needs and preferences. For example, depending on the system you use, you can purchase such inserts as church meetings, shopping lists, car maintenance schedules, city maps, and refills for the basic categories such as project planning, goals, notes, and address book pages. There is also a good personal organizer called Day-Timer that is available only by mail-order (800-556-5430). Personal organizers can be expensive, but you get what you pay for—if you use them!

55 ring binder

One advantage of using a three- or six-ring binder organizing system like Day Runner or Filofax is that you choose to carry with you only what you need. If you use a ring binder, think light. For example, carry only one or two months of your daily appointment calendar. For long-range planning, use a small foldout yearly calendar or a monthly calendar that takes up no more than six two-sided sheets. When you add a new month to the binder, transfer any plans to it from the yearly calendar, and remove an old month.

56 think small

Good personal organizers like Filofaxes and Day Runners come in a variety of sizes. Choose the smallest one that meets your needs. Remember, if it becomes indispensable to you, you'll probably be carrying it around a lot. On the other hand, if you use a personal organizer only at work, choose a large, spacious one that will stay on your desk.

57 month by month

Success's Timesetter, Day-Timer's Wire-Bound Pocket Editions, and Keith Clark's Pocket Office are three examples of excellent month-by-month alternatives to a yearly calendar or personal organizer, recommended especially for a busy executive who doesn't want to carry around a year's worth of lists and appointments. Each system consists of twelve roomy but compact books, containing one month's worth of appointments, lists, and expenses. When the month is over, the book gets filed neatly in a box tabbed by month. At the end of the year, these books can serve as contemporaneous diaries to satisfy the IRS requirements for tax deductions.

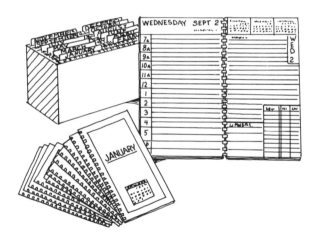

58 appointment books

Appointment books, as opposed to personal organizers, are simply compact, transportable schedule-keepers that can be used for tax, business, and/or social purposes. They can be set up to show only a day at a time, or a week, or a month, or the entire year—or some combination of them all. Two popular lines available at your office supply dealer are Success and At-a-Glance. Success products are especially well made, and beautifully designed. If you can't find them at your office supply dealer or department store, call 800-888-8488 for a mail-order catalog.

59 uses for an extra address book

If your appointment book or personal organizer comes with an address book, and you're perfectly happy with the one you already have, there are several ways to put the extra address book to good use:

1. Turn it into a vocabulary builder. Every time you come across a new word, list it alphabetically and then, the first chance you get, look it up and add the definition.
2. Use it as a multiple project planner. Alphabetize your projects and "file" your ideas in your book.
3. Keep directions to places you visit periodically.

60 year after year

Just before a new year starts, transfer all of your yearly due dates and events to the new year's appointment book or calendar. Use a single brightly colored pen for this task so the notations will be easy to recognize when you transfer them again at the end of the current year. Among these dates, include tax payments, car registration and license renewals, important birthdays and anniversaries, yearly trips and conferences, and your own birthday—unless, of course, you want to forget it.

61 mark the day

Whether you use a daily, weekly, or monthly appointment calendar, use a bookmark at the current page so you won't have to riffle through several pages to find it. A small pen that won't destroy the binding serves as a handy bookmark for this purpose.

62 what's on for tomorrow?

To avoid oversleeping or finding yourself unprepared for an important appointment, check your next day's schedule in your appointment book before you go to sleep. Then glance at the page again in the morning.

63 advance warning

Use your appointment calendar to remind yourself to prepare for appointments, when necessary. For example, for every entry that says, "Report due," there should be at least one preceding it saying, "Write report." When you write an entry such as "Call accountant," include one or more reminding yourself to "Prepare figures for accountant." Allow generous blocks of time for such tasks.

64 tickler files

Set up a series of twelve folders, one for each month of the year, starting with the current month. Put extra copies of notes, memos, and correspondence that will need to be attended to at a certain time in the appropriate month's file. Also include other things, such as regular bills you don't receive invoices for, people to call, books to order, or when mail-order items are due to arrive. File originals in permanent files and not in tickler files. When the task is done, destroy the tickler copy. If the tickled task is not done in the current month, reschedule it by moving the reminder to a later file.

65 portable permanence

Large desk diaries are recommended only for people whose work and home life are truly 100% separate. Portable personal organizers and appointment calendars are far more versatile, and they can double as desk diaries when you're at work. If you need to have your appointments or lists visible as you work, prop your organizer on an acrylic stand or book holder, and don't forget to take it home when you leave every day.

66out-of-towners

Whether for business or pleasure, if you make an appointment to see people from out of town, find out where they'll be staying and request the phone number (or look it up, if it's a hotel). Put the information in your appointment book so you will be able to cancel, confirm, or change plans without relying on them to contact you.

67confirm the confirmation

If you make an appointment that you need to confirm well ahead of time, make a note in your appointment book on the confirmation date. Include the phone number so you won't have to look it up.

68maybe, maybe not

Use pencil in your appointment book for tentative dates or alternative dates. Erase canceled tentative dates and pen over or circle the pencil when a tentative date becomes definite.

69two calendars

If your home life and office life don't overlap, keep two calendars, one at home and one at work. In your home calendar, record birthdays, when to change the oil in the car, when to change the water filter, and other household reminders. The work calendar should contain only work-related notations or appointments you'll need to remember while you're at work, such as a weekday dentist appointment. When you need to be double sure, make an entry on both calendars.

70 one calendar

If you prefer to carry only one calendar or appointment book for work and home, use one that divides your day into time zones. If your schedule isn't too complicated, keep work related items on the top of the page and home notes and appointments on the bottom. If it helps, draw a diagonal line across each part of the day as it passes to separate home from work entries.

71 digital diaries

If you're tired of crossing out names in your phone book, searching through last names that begin with *S*, and squeezing new numbers into overfilled pages, go to an electronics store and investigate the latest digital diaries. The better models can store more than enough names and numbers for most people's needs, allow you to erase, correct, and move incorrect or outdated entries, and alphabetize automatically as you make additions and changes. Light, compact, and easy to carry, digital diaries are great for making lists. Some have a function for storing credit card numbers, bank card numbers, and other secret codes. Others will keep your schedule, too, and coordinate it with a built-in calendar. Even if you prefer to keep your schedule manually in a separate nonelectronic appointment book, a digital diary is worth having for the telephone and memo capabilities. Casio, Sharp, Hewlett-Packard, and Rolodex are just four of the many companies that make such products. Test them all and see which one best suits your needs.

72 executive class

If you're already using a digital diary and find that it satisfies your personal needs but not your growing business needs, consider stepping up. Much like the personal digital diary but far more powerful, the business digital diary is light enough to carry, or it can sit open on your desk and replace your address card file, personal organizer, and appointment calendar. Some offer interchangeable R.A.M. cards that can expand functions and turn the diary into an electronic dictionary; legal, financial, or medical dictionary; expense manager; and spreadsheet. Many can also be linked to your computer if you need to generate printed lists and reports. It's relatively easy to learn how to use a business digital diary, but they are not for the computer-phobic. As with all electronic data organizers, it's a good idea to keep a backup hard copy of important data.

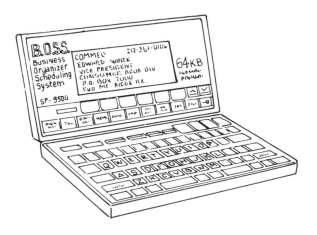

BATHROOM

73 makeup magic

If you can't find what you need for organizing stray bathroom items in a bath shop, look in an office supply or art store for acrylic organizers and caddies. You may find just what you need to separate compacts instead of notepads, eyebrow pencils instead of lead pencils, lipsticks instead of magic markers, tubes of cream or toothpaste instead of tubes of paint, and so on.

74 cabinet fever

Open your bathroom cabinet. If it looks messy or is jammed with heaven knows what, empty it completely. Throw out anything with an expired date and all perishables over a year old: over-the-counter products, medicines, prescriptions, toiletries, and cosmetics. Even toothpaste expires; the expiration date is on the crimp of the tube.

75 one at a time

If you have an unreasonably large nail polish, perfume, or lipstick collection, pare it down. Get rid of the ones you'll never use and sort the remaining items by category and color. Use any duplicate or closely similar supplies one at a time until you have only one of each item left. Replace each element of your streamlined collection as you use it up.

76 shower caddy

No bathroom should be without a shower caddy. A shower caddy is a plastic-covered wire shelf that fits over the shower head or attaches with suction cups to the tile walls. It allows easy access to soaps, shaving cream, lotions, conditioners, razors, and anything else you might want in the shower.

77 "towel" rack

If you have a large bathroom, consider adding a standing coat rack. It will not only enhance the decor in an unusual way but will be quite useful for hanging guest towels and robes. Some coat racks have small extensions that jut out near the bottom and can be used for drying wet shoes. Coat racks can be nice additions in guest rooms and bedrooms, too.

78 hair today

Consider installing a single wire shelf in your bathroom for toiletries such as powders, sprays, and creams that you use every day. Hang a simple *S*-hook from the side of the shelf, and hang your hair dryer from the hook (make sure you buy a hair dryer with a loop for hanging). *S*-hooks can be found in any hardware store.

79 bathroom magnet

Attach a long, straight magnet to the back of your medicine chest to neatly hold scissors, tweezers, clippers, shavers, and other metal objects.

BEDROOM

30under the bed

Make good use of under-bed space. Buy Rubbermaid clear plastic storage boxes with snap-on lids for dust-free, long-term underbed storage of seasonal clothing and other things you want access to infrequently. They come in many sizes and allow you to see what's inside. If you like, attach casters to the bottom, so they will roll under and out easily.

31the right start

Get into the habit of making the bed in the morning. It's very rewarding. In only a few seconds, you can make the whole room feel fresh and neat. It provides inspiration for the rest of the day and an orderly nest for a peaceful repose when you return.

CAR

32how do I get there again?

Do you find you ask for the same directions over and over? That's an embarrassing, annoying waste of time for you, and for the direction giver. You would only have to ask once if you kept an active "directions" file at home. Every time you take down directions put them in the file. Keep a local or state map in the file, too.

33driving time

To determine how long your trip will take, all you

need to know is how far you are from your destination and how fast you're going to drive. Divide the miles per hour (use the speed limit minus five as an estimate unless you expect traffic or tend to drive even slower) by the miles in the trip. The result will be your driving time. If you're traveling fifty miles on a road that has a fifty-five-mile-per-hour speed limit, you can use the formula to estimate your trip at one hour. If you intend to stop for any reason, add the stopped time to the total trip time.

84 lots to remember

When you park your car in a daily parking lot or garage, be sure to get a claim ticket and always put it in the same safe place, such as with your credit cards or money. Check that the address of the lot is on the ticket or make a note of the location. Do not leave valuables in the car, and check that you have complied with the regulations of the lot as to whether and where to leave your keys. If the keys are in the ignition, don't lock the door! If you can't remember all this, keep a checklist in your glove compartment.

85 vehicle maintenance

Every time you service your car, note the place and type of service and the current mileage on a chart in your glove compartment. Also note the next recommended service date in your appointment calendar.

86 car conscientious

Waiting until your car breaks down to find a mechanic is a bad idea. Don't add to your troubles by becoming a "hostage" to high prices and arrogant service in the midst of an emergency. If you don't have a good mechanic, comparison-shop and line one up now or right before you become a car owner.

87 no-junk trunk

Keep an emergency kit in the trunk of your car. Include a flashlight, a first-aid kit, a snow scraper and brush, a lock deicer, a tightly closed plastic container filled with water, an empty plastic container, a tire inflater, an extra can of oil, windshield washer fluid, and of course everything you need to change a tire, including a good spare.

88 trunk wise and schlepp foolish

If you regularly drive to an activity that requires equipment and your trunk space allows, don't take the equipment back and forth from your home to the car. Leave it in the trunk. For example, leave your beach chairs in the trunk, at least during the summer months. Leave your tennis equipment there, too, provided the trunk isn't damp, humid, or too cold.

89 glove compartment

Here's a checklist for your glove compartment: a valid insurance certificate, sunglasses, a local map, a car manual, a driving-club list of services and repair procedures, pen and pad, a car maintenance record and calendar, auto discount coupons, a flashlight, and, if you use them, driving gloves. Never leave your car registration card in the glove compartment. If someone were to steal the car and get caught, they'd have proof of ownership.

90 spare change

Hide change in the car for meters and emergency phone calls. If you don't smoke, use the ashtray.

91 car clip

It's almost essential to keep a pad and pencil in the car. You can keep them in your glove compartment, but you'll find them much more useful if you purchase a pad that attaches to your dashboard with Velcro. Better yet, buy a clip that holds the pad as well as loose pieces of paper, such as directions or the day's driving receipts.

92 auto office

Rubbermaid's Auto Office Seat Desk System, available at most office product dealers, is a godsend for highly mobile executives and traveling salespeople who tend to ride solo. A large but lightweight multicompart-mented portable desk and cabinet system, the Auto Office fits into the passenger seat with the seatbelt holding it in place. A large compartment conceals calculators. stereo equipment, tape recorders, car phones, and other valuable portables. A side compart-ment stores pens, pencils, notepads, and paper clips. A file compartment holds schedules, reports, and files (including hanging files if you add the optional modular file-bin accessory). To top it all off, it has a swiveling clipboard and a carrying strap for transporting the desk to your trunk or home.

93 clue handle

Attach a Post-it or tape a note to your car door handle reminding you to shut off the lights, take the keys, empty the trunk, remove the tape deck, or anything else you tend to forget or fear forgetting.

94 on the road again

Whether you travel to work by car or train, whether you're the driver or the passenger, you can make good use of commute time. Provided it doesn't affect your driving concentration, instead of listening to the radio, listen to educational or inspirational tapes or dictate ideas, plans, memos, and letters into a tape recorder that doesn't need to be held and activates only when you speak.

95 buying a used car

Decide what you want to spend. List your requirements (e.g. air conditioning, cruise control, four doors). Study a buyer's guide to used-car shopping (Consumers Union, publishers of *Consumer Reports*, sells a good annual edition). Determine the kind of car you want based on your budget, the book's recommendations, and your personal needs. Make a list of cars that fit the bill. Search for those specific cars.

96 stereo to go

If you have a removable car radio, cassette, or compact disc player, and you don't think it will be safe in the trunk, make provisions to carry it with you. You don't want to walk around the streets with it in your hands. Select a padded shoulder bag that's just big enough to house it securely and comfortably, and leave the bag in the glove compartment (or in the trunk if your glove compartment is full) until you're ready to remove the equipment.

97 where's my timer?

Do you park at meters often? Do you get tickets because you forget to return to put in more money? Here's a solution: a one-hour parking timer designed to alert you when it's time to feed the meter. Meter timers are available at many hardware and auto stores. If you can't find one, a small kitchen timer will work as well. Keep your timer in the glove compartment, and make a mental note to retrieve it when you park at a meter. Or if you have one, set your watch alarm. Whatever you use, don't think you can skip it because you'll "only be a minute."

98 eyes on the road, hands on the wheel

If you have a car phone, remember that organized means safe. There are hundreds of items available from office supply dealers, auto stores, organization stores, and catalogs that help protect the lives of cellular-car-phone owners. Some of the smartest are a cellular headset or neck cradle that allows you to keep your head straight and your hands on the wheel; a clip called an Auto Note that attaches to your windshield, holds a pen, pad, and phone numbers, and lights up so you can read it easily at night; and a sun visor directory, another item that provides quick and easy access to phone numbers.

CLOTHING

99 start from scratch

If your bedroom closet is filled with clutter, the first thing to do is empty it. Before deciding whether to install new shelves or make other adjustments, take a hard look at the items you have removed. The idea is to get rid of the old, out-of-style stuff that doesn't even fit you. Enlist a friend to help—someone who can be brutally honest, and whose opinion you trust. A good rule of thumb for those with limited space: If you haven't worn it in the past year, get rid of it.

100 closet depth

A standard closet is twenty-four inches deep. A too-shallow closet won't hold your clothes neatly, but a closet that's too deep can cause problems too. If you install a hanging bar toward the back of a deep closet, you have to walk into the closet to reach your clothes, and you may tend to throw things on the floor in front of them, creating a mess. If you position the hanging bar too far forward, you lose the space in the back, and things may fall there, never to be found again. The solution: Design your closet with a *U* shape in mind to make the best use of the space on the sides of the closet as well as the back. If necessary, add a raised platform toward the front for shoes or stepping up.

101 three piles: the "no's"

Separate everything in your closet into three piles: the yes's, the maybe's, and the no's. Donate the wearable or salvageable no's to charity, or take them to a consignment shop that will sell your hand-me-downs and give you a share of the profits. Recycle or discard the rest.

102 three piles: the "maybe's"

Go through the maybe's. Try them on. What's wrong? What's right? Why haven't you worn this piece of clothing in ten years, and why won't you part with it? Is it out of style? Do you feel good when you put it on? Is it your color? Does it need mending? Would you wear it if you mended it? Try to reduce your maybe pile by at least half. Put the rest in a marginal pile for one month. If, after a month, you haven't worn an item or even missed it, put it in the no pile and dispose of it.

103 three piles: the "yes's"

Next, consider the clothes you want to keep. Measure everything you have to determine your needs, and then measure your closet space to determine how it can best meet them. Make a list of the number of long hanging garments such as dresses and coats, the number of suits, shirts, belts, gloves, shoes, and so on. Do you need to change your shelving system? Add a second level? Do you want to put in sliding baskets? Try to arrange the space so that all of the air in the closet is used while everything is kept separate, accessible, untangled, and easy to identify. Visit a closet or organizing shop. Many companies make beautiful custom closet organization systems, these include Lee/Rowan, Stanley, Artwire, CSD, Elfa, and Heller. Only you can decide which system best suits your space, needs, and budget.

104 shoes, shoes, shoes

It would take 500 pages to fully describe all the shoe storage products available. Go to an organizing or houseware store and you'll find shoe bars, bags, boxes, and shelves, designed to go in the closet, over the door, in the corner, or under the bed. Count your shoes, measure the space you have to store them in, and then pick out something that does the job. The ideal system will store your shoes neatly, while seeing that they remain accessible. Hygiene is a concern, too; remember that the bottoms of your shoes come in contact with lots of grime. Shoe racks should be airy and cleanable. When choosing your shoe storage system, allow room for growth, and try to use air and wall space, as well as floor space.

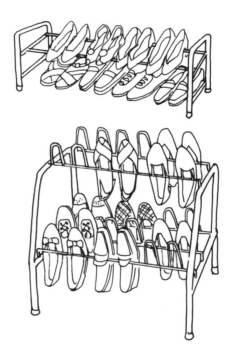

105 sweater storage

During warm weather, sweaters can be easily stored in see-through snap-shut plastic boxes such as those made by Rubbermaid, or in see-through, vinyl sweater bags. Both options keep them neat, dust-free, and static-free and protect them from pulling. Sweaters can be stored in boxes or bags while they're in season too, but don't pack them in too tightly. You'll save time folding as well as wear and tear on your sweaters if you store each one separately or in groups of two.

106 new season's clothes

Separate your clothing by season. When you think the weather has changed more-or-less permanently, take a few hours to make the switch. Put the new season's clothes where they will be accessible, and store away clothes you won't need in the coming months.

107 make ready

When clothes come back from the dry cleaners, don't just throw the whole batch into the closet. Remove the tie twist; remove the plastic so your clothes can breathe, separate garments by type, length, season, and color; and sort them in your well-organized closet. If you can convince your dry cleaner to use less wrapping material and fewer hangers, your job will be that much easier, and the environment will be that much better off.

108 hose tricks

Shoe bags that hang on the closet wall aren't the best way to store shoes. But clear shoe bags are great for storing bulky socks and hosiery! Try it.

109 no tight closets

To save room in your out-of-season closet, put several blouses or shirts of one color on a single hanger. This is not a recommended storage technique for items you use every day.

110 the hanger, too

When you take a hanging item out of the closet, take out the hanger, too. Remove the garment, place the empty hanger on one side of the closet, and push the remaining clothes toward the other side. This keeps hangers neat and accessible. Donate excess hangers to a dry cleaner or laundry service.

111 detangler

Tangled hangers should not be accepted as a fact of life. Many closet organizing systems and accessories include hanger separators that keep space between adjacent hangers. What a relief.

112 hosiery drawers

Roll hosiery up to store it. Keep the balls neat, and keep like colors together. In a drawer, put hosiery of the same color in a line from front to back. When taking a pair out to wear, if all else is equal, select the first in a line and then move the whole line forward. Whenever you put clean hosiery back into the drawer, put it in the back. This keeps everything in the drawer in circulation. If you never use the items in the back, they'll deteriorate. Not only is this a waste, but anything you don't use shouldn't be taking up room in your drawer.

113 top drawer

Most people keep their undergarments in the top drawer, and it's a good idea because it's usually the handiest place. The top drawers throughout your home should contain frequently used items.

114 drawer plan

Everyday or often-used items should be kept handy. If you find you're always bending down to get your belt and then have to walk across the room to get your shirt, rethink your drawer plan. Put the items you use most often near each other and as close to waist height or eye level as possible.

115 under pare

Do you dread your underwear drawer every day? If so, it's probably full of old, disorganized garments, many of which are of marginal use. Add sectional drawer organizers, and throw out anything you haven't worn in so long that the elastic crackles.

116 jewelry deco

If your necklaces and bracelets are pretty enough to hang on your body, they're pretty enough to hang on the wall. Arrange hooks in a symmetrical pattern on your bedroom wall and use them to hang your necklaces and bracelets. Not only will the jewelry look decorative, but it will stay untangled. If you don't want your display to be so prominent, place the hooks on a wall inside your closet or behind your bedroom door.

117 vertical organizers for jewels

There are endless products designed to organize jewelry. Those with compartments are usually best. You can use an ice-cube tray in your drawer, but you're better off getting an organizer that uses more vertical than horizontal space, particularly if you keep your jewelry on a bureau top or dressing table.

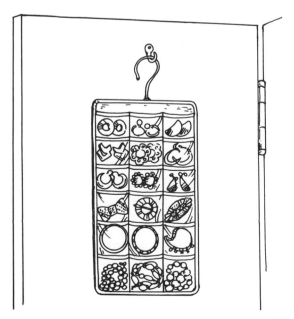

118 night dish

Keep a bowl or dish—preferably one with compartments—in your night table drawer or top dresser drawer, or on top of your dresser. A night dish is the best place to keep all those items you keep on your person from morning until night and remove only when you sleep: your watch and ring, other jewelry, keys, wallet, change, and so on. There's no sense in putting these things in ten different places every night only to have to collect them again the next morning.

119 so sew

Don't let your sewing basket pile up for so long that the clothes go out of style. Before you do spend time or money sewing, however, ask yourself whether you will use the repaired item because, if you won't, don't bother to fix it at all; dispose of it at once by giving it away, recycling it, or throwing it out. If you have something to sew, sew it the next time you have a few minutes, or take it to the tailor the next time you are going that way.

120 not just for children

Sew a long piece of yarn between each pair of gloves or mittens and run it through your coat inside and out both sleeves. You'll never lose your gloves again.

121 the night before

If you want to be sure to look presentable in the morning, or if you just want a few minutes of extra sleep, make it a habit to plan your next day's wardrobe the night before. Assemble your entire outfit, including accessories, and hang it on a hook behind your bedroom door, or put it all on one side of your closet, or lay it out on a dressing table.

122 season's colors

Try to organize each season's wardrobe around a color group that is fashionable and that complements your complexion and personality. This will help make you a more focused shopper and will allow you to create more outfits from fewer clothes—thus saving time, money, and space in your closet.

123 swap shop

Organize a clothing swap party for you and your friends—preferably before you've all done your shopping for a new season. Invite your friends to bring clothes they never wear and have fun laughing, trading, and trying on. After everyone has made their selections, pack up what's left for charity.

COLLECTIONS

124 room to grow

No matter what you're collecting—compact disks, books, photos, stamps, coins—if you intend to add to the collection, choose a storage system that allows for expansion. To be doubly sure, buy twice the amount of display or storage capacity you currently need. Not only will this save you shopping time, but it will also save you the frustration of looking for out-of-stock or discontinued storage items.

125 knickknack paddywack

When you own a lot of knickknacks, you take on the responsibility of arranging them on a shelf, dusting them, and rearranging them after they've been dusted. Keep that in mind before you start accumulating a large collection. But once you own them, one way to remember where they go is to stick adhesive-backed colored dots on the shelf and apply matching colored dots to the bottom of the collectibles. Don't do this if you're concerned about the finish on your shelf.

126 unusual display

Have a piece of glass cut to fit over the top of your bureau, coffee table, side table, or kitchen table. Not only will the glass protect the furniture and wipe clean easily, but if you like, you can display photos and other collections, such as pretty stamps or postcards underneath, and the glass will protect them too!

127 specialized collections

If you own a lot of collectibles, consider subscribing to magazines that specialize in those subjects; magazines will offer ideas on how to arrange your collections, how to improve them, how to appraise them, and where to sell them. Magazines may even help you establish friendships with others who share your interest.

128 plastic portfolios

Ask your art or office supply dealer to show you a selection of loose-leaf vinyl-paged portfolios and presentation folders such as those made by Duo-Tang, Lion Office Products, and Itoya. They're perfect for storing and displaying photos, negatives, baseball cards, certificates, recipes, documents, magazine clippings, stamp collections, and other loose, flat items. Label the spines, and keep your portfolios upright on a bookshelf.

129 photo cut

Here's a clever way to organize your photos that makes them more interesting to look at: Find a photo album with slightly adhesive pages covered with one large sheet of plastic. Carefully cut around the important subjects in each photo, leaving out all the extraneous background material. Arrange your photos on the page in a way that pleases you. Make people from two different photos look at each other, for example, or overlay the photos slightly to make a collage. If you like, complete the arrangements by writing descriptions on scraps of pretty, lightly colored wrapping paper or Avery labels.

130 don't wait

When you get photos back from processing, take the time to jot down who, what, when, and where on the back of the photos—or on the page if you're putting them in an album—while the pictures are still fresh in your mind. Your notes will spark memories and give you more to talk about while you're reminiscing with friends or loved ones.

131 shoot and print

If you really want to be organized about taking photographs, keep a pen and notebook in your camera bag. Every time you take a picture, record the number of the picture, the date, the place, and the subject. It's a foolproof method of keeping track of your photos, and the list doubles as a travel diary. When the pictures have been developed, keep them in order, and look at them beside your list. Transfer any relevant notes to the backs of the pictures or to your album. Or keep the photo record in the album, followed by the pictures.

COMMUNICATIONS

132 don't hang up

Some people think it's rude to screen calls with an answering machine. Other people, including myself, see screening calls as a timesaving, organizing tool that lets a person decide when to speak on the telephone. Why is it less rude to interrupt someone with a call without notice and expect him or her to spend time attending to your needs? Conversely, if you leave a message on a machine, let the person know the best time to return your call, so you won't be interrupted while you're busy.

133 action, take one

Make your announcement message on your answering machine as short as you can so it doesn't waste time when people call you, and encourage them to do the same when leaving you a message. Plan what you're going to say before you say it and write it out. Tape the script to the bottom of the machine in case the message gets erased or in case you want to change your message to something completely different temporarily.

134 avoid phone tag

Include a request on your answering machine announcement that callers leave a number where they can be reached and the best time for you to call them back.

135 action, take two

Most message tapes have two sides. If possible, tape the B side when you tape the A side—with an alternate message, such as the one you would like callers to hear when you are out of town. You may also want to play a different message during the week than you do on the weekend.

136 number please

When you leave a message on an answering machine, be sure to leave your phone number, the time of day, and the best time to reach you. Many people call in to their machines to hear their messages and don't have phone numbers handy. You're more likely to get a prompt response if you leave your number.

137 at the beep

If you're at work and you want to remember to make a call when you get home, just call your answering machine and leave yourself a message. You can leave yourself other messages too, such as things you want to do that night or stories you want to remember to tell people at home. Chances are you'll check your machine as soon as you get home.

138 just the fax, ma'am

Prepare a fax transmittal form to use as a cover sheet when sending faxes. Make it very simple. It should include your address and phone number, your fax number, and the recipient's fax number, the number of pages being faxed (including the cover sheet), and a place for a short cover message.

139 slow time

When you're between projects, fill out fax transmittal

forms to people you send frequent faxes. Fill out as much of each form as you can, photocopy it, and keep the copies near your fax machine. You'll have that much less to do when you're rushing to get a fax out.

140 fax tracks

Either preprogram frequently called numbers into your fax machine or tape a list of numbers you use often on or near the machine. If the list is long, reduce it several times on your photocopy machine.

141 Muzak to my ears

A speakerphone with an automatic redial feature is a terrific organizing device. If you're put on hold, you can walk away from the Muzak until you hear the sound of a human voice. Redial is helpful when you're calling a busy number. Don't go too far, keep your ears open, and when you hear "Hello," be quick.

142 on the phone

If your time is scarce, use it efficiently. Make a list of mindless chores and do them while you're talking on the phone. Cordless phones are best for this purpose, but there are tasks you can do from your chair, too, such as sticking stamps on envelopes, sorting paper clips, or polishing your nails. If you have a cordless, however, you can even sort the laundry. No one has to know.

143 telephone objectives

Keep a telephone-objective memo pad near your phone. Make it a habit to note the purpose of your calls before you make them so the conversation goes smoothly and you don't forget something and need to call back.

144 after the beep

When you leave a message on someone's answering machine, make a note on your telephone-objective memo. Beside the entry for that person, write the letters *MSG* to indicate to yourself that you left a message. Because your telephone-objective memo is always kept beside the phone, you'll be able to speak to the person when they return your call in an organized fashion. When you're finished speaking, cross the name off your list. If necessary, transfer the person's phone number to your telephone directory or Rolodex.

145 lots of queries

Before you call any business with a complicated question or a series of questions—whether you're shopping around, need something repaired, or want to hire someone to perform a service for you—especially if you're calling a busy establishment, make a list of questions you want to ask in order of importance. When you get on the phone, the first thing you should say is, "I have a few questions, please." If you ignore this rule and jump right into your first question ("Where are you located?"), you risk being answered with "At Main and Maple. Click." Then you'll have to call back, and—if you can get through again—you'll be lucky to get the time of day.

146 bill check

Keep a log of your long-distance phone calls near the phone. When the bill arrives, check it against the list. Also, *Bottom Line* (1-800-274-5611), a bimonthly newsletter filled with great organizing, financial, health, and other ideas and resources, recommends that you "have your phone bill audited." They explain, "Some long-distance companies offer auditing services. You send them several monthly bills and they determine what you would have paid had you used their service. Have your long-distance bill audited by several different firms, and choose the least expensive." They add, "Rates change…have your bill audited at least once a year."

147 get the lowdown

If you make a lot of phone calls, keep in mind that rates are different at different times of the day and on the weekends. Find out exactly when the rates change and keep the information near your phone. Whenever it is convenient, make your calls when the cost is as low as possible.

148 do what you will

Your white pages and yellow pages are your own personal organizing tools. They belong to you. You can write in them, highlight them, add Post-its to them. Circle numbers you look up regularly. Cross out numbers of hated establishments to avoid ever calling again. Correct incorrect listings. You can even tear out charts that you use a lot, and hang them on your bulletin board. They're free, and they're yours.

149 call, write, or visit?

Evaluate all communications according to the time and energy required to accomplish your objectives. How can the message be transmitted best? Will a telephone call or a fax message accomplish as much as a personal visit? Will a letter accomplish as much as a telephone call? Is any contact really necessary at all?

COMPUTER

150 file-onic

Set up your computer files, disks, and directories using the same headings as you use for your hard-copy files. A computer filing system, like any filing system, is good only if you can find what you filed.

151 every day's a new day

If you need to name a file quickly or need to name a series of random or temporary files, use the day's date, including the year. To store different versions of the same document under different file names, use the date as part of the file name. That way there's little risk of repeating the file name and erasing a file. Also, when you call the file up, you'll know when it was created.

152 make room

To save space on your desk, keep some computer components on the floor. Most can be propped on their sides on the floor in a system unit stand. Just be careful that the unit is securely positioned, especially when the hard drive is in use. Computer and office supply stores sell CPU stands designed to keep the unit stationary and secure in an upright position. Caution: Sometimes it's necessary to "park" your hard drive before moving the unit. Check your manual.

153 swivel and tilt

Remember that most computer monitors these days swivel and tilt. If yours does, don't forget to tilt it into the most comfortable position for you. If it doesn't tilt and you would like it to, buy a universal swivel base. Organized means comfortable.

154 sliding drawer

If your computer is situated on a shallow tabletop, install an underdesk sliding drawer for the keyboard. It neatly holds the keyboard and keeps it off your work space. If you like, find an extra-wide drawer that will hold a mouse or notes beside the keyboard.

155 desk strategy

When you're buying a desk for your computer, make sure it's deep enough to allow you to look straight ahead over the keyboard at the monitor, instead of down, or at an angle. The keyboard should be at a comfortable height, too. Consider where you will put papers that you need to refer to while you're working, and where you'll store the system unit, the printer, disks, and books.

156 my computer does that?

If you have a computer—be it an IBM-compatible PC or a MacIntosh—have fun with it. Research software options. Try not to use your computer only for its one original purpose. Some good programs that will help organize your finances, for example, are Quicken (Intuit; 1-800-624-8742), Dome Simplified Bookkeeping System (Dome; 1-800-432-4352), MacInTax (Softview; 1-800-622-6829), and For the Record (Nolo Press; 1-415-549-1976). You can create all kinds of legal documents with It's Legal (Parsons Technology; 1-800-223-6925). You can be your own interior decorator with Instant Decorator (Abracadata Ltd.; 1-800-451-4871). You can plan meals, search for recipes, create your own cookbook, convert measurements, and generate shopping lists with Microkitchen Companion (Lifestyle Software Group; 1-800-289-1157). Pic Trac Photo Management System (Glacier Software; 1-800-234-5026) organizes, identifies, and labels enormous photo and slide collections. Prepare detailed flowcharts for new projects with Everybody's Planner (Abracadata Ltd.; 1-800-451-4871). Improve your writing, learn French—there's almost no limit to what you can do on your computer—with the right software. *Warning: Some software systems require more memory to operate than others. Be sure you purchase software that will work with your system.*

157 organizonic

There are many excellent software programs for both IBM-compatible and MacIntosh systems specifically designed to keep you organized. Two of the best are Sidekick (Borland; 1-800-331-0877) and Desqview (Quarterdeck; 1-213-392-9851). More than just electronic organizers, these programs organize your personal or network computer environment as well. Both programs have appointment calendars, scheduling, and calculator capabilities, notepads for making lists and memos, and the ability to enhance your computer's multitask capability. They allow you to work at one task in the foreground, such as planning a schedule, while the computer is working at a completely different task in the background, such as computing a financial analysis. These programs have address books and an automatic speed dialer to call people through your modem. Sidekick also has an alarm that you can use to remind yourself to do something—such as make a call or take medication—whether the computer is on or off!

158 keyboard shortcuts

Over the long run, you'll save a lot of time if you minimize the number of keystrokes you use to perform a function—especially functions you use frequently. There are almost always at least two ways to perform each task. Take the time to learn shortcuts that will help you work more efficiently. You'll be glad you did.

159 macros

Most word-processing programs have the capacity to call up frequently used copy blocks such as addresses and salutations with only one to three keys. It's worth learning these advanced capabilities and incorporating them into your daily routine. Every keystroke saved is a second earned. They add up fast.

160 printer stand pluses

If you can find one, get a printer stand that does double duty as a storage station. At the very least, a good printer stand should be able to hold the printer paper in use as well as an extra box, and it must have a place to collect printed paper. In addition, look for one that has a pull-out drawer for safely housing diskettes (in the size or sizes you use) and perhaps a shelf for manuals and program boxes.

161off the desk

Copyholders—desk accessories designed to let you look straight ahead at a piece of paper—have evolved considerably and no longer take up valuable work space. The best copyholders attach to the side of a computer monitor or typewriter, adjust to any angle, and can be mounted on either the right or the left. The most versatile and inconspicuous copyholder I've found is BC's "Robotic Arm" Universal Mini Copy Holder 200 (long name, compact product), but others include the Curtis Clip and the SRW copyholder.

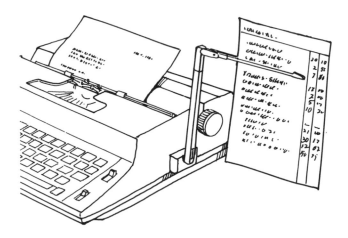

162disk organization

Use the color-coded labels that come in a box of diskettes to label your floppies. If possible, use one color for utilities, one for each database, one for each word-processing or desktop program, and another for documents. Label all disks carefully with a felt-tipped pen. Document disk labels should include the program used to create the document and whether the disk is high density or low density, if the manufacturer has not already marked the disk. Keep floppies in a dust-free disk holder, with the disks you use most often in the front. Arrange the sections of the disk holder by color.

163 floppies sloppy?

If you use DOS and floppy disks, every once in a while, print a directory of what's on your floppy disks using the dir/w command. If you have a MacIntosh, use "Print Directory" under the "File" menu. Reduce the printed pages on a photocopy machine, cut them into small squares, and tuck them into the floppy disk holder or tape them neatly to the outside of the disk holder for quick reference. You may find it helpful to post the directories of your most-often-used disks on a bulletin board near the computer.

164 avoid a crash

Get a surge protector. Power sources are contaminated and uneven. You don't want to lose data. Power surge protectors also allow you to plug lots of equipment in and help keep wires tidy. For easy recognition, attach labels to the surge protector to identify the plugs.

ENTERTAINMENT

165 oh, the tray

If you're serving food and beverages, or eating by yourself, in a room other than the kitchen, don't make several trips back and forth to serve, and then again to clean up. Remember to use a tray!

166 where to sit

Set the table before guests arrive. If you want to control where people sit, put out place cards. To encourage particular people to talk to each other at a long, narrow table, seat them opposite each other; at a wide or round table, seat them next to each other.

167 for our guests

Keep local guidebooks, maps, and restaurant reviews and menus for your out-of-town house guests. They'll appreciate having bus and subway information, and other schedules, too. If you have time before they arrive, you can even stop by a local hotel and pick up a few fliers describing sights and current happenings.

168 open house

For an all-day party or open house, plan to serve foods that will not spoil at room temperature. Serve them in large bowls that can be refilled easily and keep extra bowls handy for serving food brought by guests.

169 easy serve

Ask your guests for any diet restrictions when you invite them. If it's impossible to ask everyone, think healthy and vegetarian. Then plan the meal to allow you as much time as possible with your guests. Hot hor d'oeuvres should be ready to pop into the oven when guests arrive. Cold hors d'oeuvres should be ready to bring out. An excellent choice for a main course is a one-dish meal such as a casserole. Prepare salads ahead of time, and have side dishes ready to serve or reheat. Put beverages in a handy place so guests can help themselves, or appoint someone else to be the "beverage tender."

170 before they arrive

Before your party guests arrive, take out everything you'll need for serving, from bowls, platters, and spoons to ladles, spatulas, and cake plates. There's nothing more frustrating than having all the food prepared in advance—appetizers to desserts—and then keeping your guests waiting while you turn over the kitchen looking for a corkscrew, a cheese knife, or a pretty serving bowl.

FAMILY

171 hear ye, hear ye

Family members shouldn't have to look all over the house to see if they have messages. Create a family message center that all can check when they come in. Depending on the size of your household, the message center can be an erasable board with hanging marker on the refrigerator or a pad and pen beside a cubbyhole box in the den.

172 where's my...?

Every family member should have an "in-station" where others can deposit mail, papers, messages, and miscellaneous personal belongings.

173 organize for others

If you have elderly relatives who live alone and are sometimes forgetful about paying bills, with the relatives' permission, ask their phone and gas-and-electric companies to notify you if their check is overdue, that is *before* shutting down needed services, of course. In most cases, companies will be happy to cooperate.

174 just in case

It's important to be prepared for almost any emergency. While taking childproofing precautions, be sure your family has easy access to candles and matches, buckets, a first-aid kit, batteries, new fuses, twine, and at least one flashlight. Your circuit breaker should be carefully labeled and a flashlight kept nearby.

FILING

175 cabinet considerations

For those who always seem to be buried under stacks of letters, bills, statements and other paper, a filing cabinet or two can provide relief. Don't buy one until you know where you're going to put it and what you're going to store in it. Once you've settled the basics, you can choose the filing cabinet best suited to your needs. They come in letter and legal sizes, with any number of drawers. If you can get by with letter-size files, use them, because they take up less room. File cabinets may be lateral (files are stored side-to-side) or vertical (files are stored front-to-back). Lateral files are more attractive and provide more counter space, but they take up more floor space. The best file cabinets contain bars for hanging folders.

176 filing cabinets

What you choose to keep your home files in depends entirely on your needs. How much do you intend to save and, therefore, file? Do you have room for a filing cabinet? Where will your filing cabinet go? Will it be out of sight—say, in a closet—or will it be visible? Standard filing cabinets come with two drawers or four drawers, in letter- or legal-size widths, with or without steel bars that allow for hanging files, with drawers that lock or don't lock, and with other options. They come in steel, oak, pine, plastic, and any number of other materials and finishes. They can look old-fashioned or modern. Before you choose, decide how much filing capacity you need (allowing room for undercalculation and some growth), where you intend to put the filing cabinet, whether you want letter or legal size, what you intend to spend, and how much you want to put into setting up your filing system. Measure what you intend to file as well as the place where the cabinet or filing box will go. Buy prelabeled files or create your own system. Research and plan before you jump in.

177 hanging folders

Hanging folders are the greatest thing that ever happened to filing, but not all hanging folders are alike. Most companies produce hanging folders in a variety of colors, with plastic tags for labeling. On Pendaflex folders the tags can go in a variety of positions. Scores across the middle on both sides of the folders let you fold them outward to hold your place while filing. Other companies have different features. Anthes Universal makes alphabetical and numerical folders that are permanently attached to each other to keep papers from slipping in between them. While these files are more difficult to change, they are less expensive than Pendaflex, come prelabeled in easy-to-assemble kits, and may be more suitable for home use.

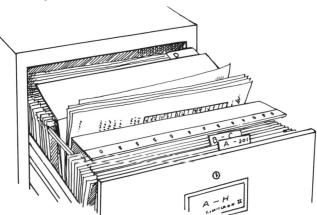

178 in the drawers

Keep your home files simple. Aim to use the fewest number of files possible that will still allow you to locate any paper you might need in seconds. Set up a series of alphabetical folders, each labeled with a single letter of the alphabet or with a group of sequential letters that do not frequently begin words and names, such as *jkl* or *xyz*. After each alphabetical folder, place specific folders for categories that contain enough material to warrant individual files. When a single category begins to take over an alphabetical folder, give it its own folder. Here are some typical home categories that might warrant their own folders: automobile; bank; bills to pay; bills paid; correspondence; deeds and certificates; education; finances; insurance; legal documents; medical; rent/mortgage; taxes; telephone; utilities.

179 the circular file

Before deciding where to file it, decide whether to file it at all. Barbara Hemphill, professional organizing consultant and author of *Taming the Paper Tiger* (Hemphill & Associates; 1-202-387-8007), points out that "80% of what goes into most people's files is never used" and recommends that you never sit down to file without having a circular file—that is, a trash basket—handy. Before filing any paper, ask yourself whether the information is available to you elsewhere, if it will become dated as it sits in the file, and what the worst consequences would be if you threw it out. If you can live with the consequences, out it goes.

180 my filing

Your filing system should make sense to you and anyone else who uses it. If an excellent system is so complicated that you can't figure it out or so simple that it doesn't allow you to sort your many papers, it is not good for you. To test your filing system, see how fast you can put your hands on a random piece of paper.

181 when in doubt

If you're the kind of person who keeps every paper, set up two files. Call one "to be filed," and the other "to be thrown." In the former, note where you expect to file each page so you don't have to read it again to file it. The latter should be set up like a tickler file—a series of folders, one for each month of the year. Put such things as offers, sales, and event announcements that will expire in these files under the month when the notice can be thrown away. When the month arrives, sort through quickly or if you can muster the courage, dump the contents without looking.

182 staple, don't clip

Don't use paper clips for keeping documents together in a file. Not only do they take up too much room, but they frequently catch on other papers and cause misfiling. Instead, staple papers together that must be attached. If you don't want to make holes in the paper, ask your office supplier for a stapleless stapler or call NAL America Co. and ask where you can get a Docu-clip (1-800-722-8806).

183 new project

Whether it's acquiring a new client or hiring a contractor, at work or at home, whenever you begin a new project, start a new folder. Put all memos, ideas, clips, correspondence, and phone notes into it. When the project is finished, pare down the file, and keep only those documents you'll need again or those you don't have access to elsewhere.

184 color chaos

Unless you perceive a real need and can invent the system, don't color-code your files. It's complicated and frustrating, and if you have a good alphabetical or numerical system, it really shouldn't be necessary. Feel free to use colorful folders, though, because they're attractive and do help you differentiate between adjacent files.

185 contract files

If your business involves contracts, choose a bright folder color, such as red, and every time you sign a contract, make a copy of it and put the copy in a folder of that color. Place these colored folders first or last in the individual client or project files—but be consistent. File the original contracts all together alphabetically or chronologically in an expanding folder, and protect them by keeping them in a fireproof safe, preferably at a different location.

186 inventory

At home and in the office, keep an inventory of your file drawers and storage closets. In the front of each file drawer, keep a list of what's in the drawer. Label the outside of boxes with a complete inventory of what's inside. Photocopy the lists and keep them in one master file that also includes where the files and boxes are located and what items are stored away in the attic, basement, and other drawers.

187 start fresh

If you can't locate something in a file, all the time you spent looking for and obtaining the item, clipping it, saving it, and filing it has been wasted. Go through your files and note all the items you have never looked back on. Then, the next time you're holding that piece of paper and thinking about where it goes, consider the trash. Now rethink your filing system.

188 warranties and manuals

Most people will benefit from a well-organized warranties and manuals file that allows them to retrieve appliance instructions and warranty information. It will come in handy whenever something breaks down, or for insurance claims, troubleshooting, and advanced instruction. Warranties and manuals are bulky, so a single folder doesn't usually do the trick; an expanding file folder with carefully labeled compartments is what you need. You can assemble one yourself, but Anthes Universal makes an expanding file that couldn't be better for this purpose. When closed, it looks like a book on a shelf, or you can put it in a filing cabinet. The compartments are labeled as follows: dishwasher; furnace/water heater; furniture; home entertainment; microwave; outdoor equipment; small appliances; stove/refrigerator; tools; vacuum cleaner; washer/dryer; and miscellaneous. With your warranties and manuals, keep serial numbers and receipts. For tax-deductible items, make a photocopy of each receipt to keep with your taxes as well.

189 home files

Keep your files all together and alphabetical. Here are some categories you may want to use: automobile, credit cards, church or synagogue, dental/medical, education, finances, gift ideas, insurance, receipts, rent/mortgage, repairs, restaurants (for keeping track of recommendations), résumé, safe deposit box, taxes, utilities, vacations, and warranties. You'll probably want to have files on a few friends and business contacts as well and one or more for your work and hobbies.

190 to be filed

Whether someone files for you or you file yourself, Post-it pads are your best friends. Before you toss a letter, report, or anything else into the "to-be-filed" box, ask yourself, "Where should this be filed?" Note your answer on a Post-it pad (or on the document itself), and attach the note to the top page. No one should have to reread something in the "to-be-filed" box to determine where to file it.

GARDEN

191 garden dimensions

Start planning your garden in the winter. Measure and lay out your yard on graph paper. Draw in the ideal garden dimensions. In the spring, when the ground is dry and you're ready to dig, use a garden hose to out-line the perimeter of the garden. A hose is ideal to use for this purpose because it's heavy enough to hold the shape but flexible enough to allow for adjustments.

192 garden color

When you're planning a flower garden, consider which

colors and flowers will look best together before you plant. Use crayons or markers on a heavy stock, or cut out colored construction paper, and map it out ahead of time. If you cut flowers for bouquets, think about what flowers would look best *inside* your home as well.

HEALTH

193 listen, doc

Before you call or visit the doctor, make a list of your symptoms and questions. Bring a pad and paper to the office and jot down any additional questions as you wait for the doctor to consult with you. Take notes when the doctor explains the diagnosis and treatment.

194 it's your body— for life

Interview your doctors and dentists. Keep records and notes: Did you like them or not? What was the cost? How did you hear of them? What did they prescribe? You can keep an extensive "medical" file if you like, but it should hold at least a careful and complete record of your own and your children's immunizations, hospitalizations, surgeries, inoculations, and diseases. These are your "medical histories." Keep medical histories for each family member on a different page so that you can bring only the one you need when you visit a new doctor.

195 extra, extra

If you're planning a trip to the hospital for an operation or to have a baby, many people will want to know what happens. Set up a "phone tree" in advance by arranging to have one or two people informed at the proper time. Those people will call two other people, and those people will call two more. Your news (good news, I hope) will be around town in a flash. And your advance planning will save your family from a sudden barrage of phone calls.

196 insurance sure

Make a chart to keep track of medical and dental insurance claims. Keep it in your "medical insurance" file along with a sample claim form, showing your insurance number and indicating how the claim needs to be filled out, and extra blank forms. On the chart, note the amount claimed, the amount billed, the name of the doctor, the procedure performed, the date of the procedure, the date of the claim, and the date of payment (to be filled in when payment arrives). A blank space in the payment column lets you know the claim is pending.

HOME DECORATING & REPAIR

197 dream

Before making decorating decisions, take a fantasy walk through your home. Can you picture your bedroom with a canopy bed and a Persian rug? Make a list. What would each room have in it if you could have anything you want. How many of those things could you have now, soon, or someday? How many of those things might you be able to improvise? Keep the list, and every once in a while...dream.

198 optimum efficiency

Now be more realistic. Take a function walk through your home (and office). How would you like each room to function? Would you like the third bedroom to be a combination guest room/TV room? Is it set up well right now to accommodate guests? Is the bed comfortable? Are guest linens handy? Do you never use the room at all? Why not? See what changes you can make so that each room of your home functions optimally.

199 picture-perfect

It's very difficult to properly organize wall arrangements on the wall. Here's a much better way, but you'll still need to be careful and take your time:

1. Pretend the floor is the wall.
2. Lay out your pictures and other wall hangings the way you want them to look on the wall.
3. Mix and match and move them around until the arrangement pleases you.
4. Measure the group's perimeter and the spaces between each picture.
5. Draw a diagram of your plan and mark all measurements carefully.
6. For accurate placement, measure the distance between the top of each picture and the center of the hanging wire when pulled taut, and position your hooks accordingly.
7. Start at one corner of your grouping, and hang one picture at a time until they're all up from the floor.

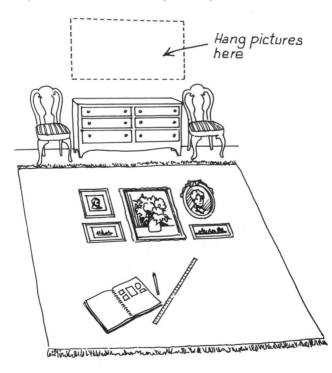

Hang pictures here

200 wireless

No matter what you do, your home is not going to look neat and attractive if you have wires streaming all over the floor. Hide wires, including wires from stereo equipment, appliances, and telephones, by hanging them in neat circles over wall hooks behind furniture. Or, if they must pass through the living area, run them along the baseboards and cover them with wire cover. Wire covers come in assorted colors, can be cut to size, and are available in most houseware and hardware stores. For safety, never run electric cords through doorways, under carpets, or in trafficked areas where they are likely to be walked on or tripped over.

201 decorating notebook

Depending on the extent of your decorating plan or renovation, start with one or more three-ring binders or portfolios with lots of blank pages and pockets. Separate the sections into useful categories, such as budgets, contractors, stores, ideas, fabrics, recommendations, and designs. As you research ideas in catalogs, magazines, and stores, clip what appeals to you and put it into your book. Add swatches, prices, sale information, phone numbers, measurements, floor plans, and sketches. This system will help your plan develop, and it can also be a lot of fun.

202 what color?

If you can't decide on colors for a carpet or upholstery, buy a big box of crayons and drawing paper, and try a variety of colors; mix and match. Or use colored construction paper and scissors. And you thought kindergarten was a waste of time.

203 floor plan

A floor plan is an indispensable tool when you're decorating a new home. Keep the floor plan with you at all times, especially while you're shopping. But first check to make sure the measurements are accurate, and note whether the room widths and depths include closet space. Fill in measurements that are not indicated on the diagram, such as window widths and heights, ceiling heights, and closet sizes. After you finish decorating, keep your floor plan safe. It will become indispensable again when you redecorate.

204 Stanley Home Planners

Stanley Tools makes a line of wonderful project designer planners for decorating and redecorating your home, office, and yard. Easy and fun to use, they consist of a graphlike board for laying out your floor plan and removable vinyl replicas of every conceivable type of furniture, ornament, and fixture. You can move around furniture and also play with the idea of adding and deleting walls. Most people have trouble imagining what an empty room would look like with furniture or how furniture would look if it were added, moved, or removed. Stanley Home Planners really help you visualize decorating schemes and renovation plans.

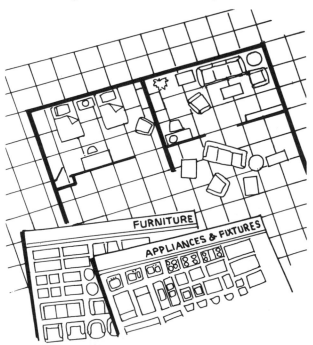

205 before and after

When renovating or redecorating, take before-and-after photographs. If you're redecorating yourself, take the before pictures with you when choosing fabrics, colors, and designs. If your home is undergoing a major renovation, the before-and-after pictures could prove useful as proof of capital improvements for tax purposes.

206 on-line design

Abracadata Ltd. (1-800-451-4871) makes a line of software products for most IBM-compatible and MacIntosh computers that you can use to design and decorate your home or office or landscape your yard on the screen. Move around heavy furniture with your little finger. You can use these programs to design your dream house from scratch, too.

207 repair goals

Go through your home with a notebook. Stand in the center of each room and look around—*really* look. Say to yourself, "What do I want to change or repair in here?" For each room, make a list of short-, medium-, and long-term goals. An example of a short-term goal: "That picture would look better hung a little lower." A medium goal: "I need a new towel-rack" or "that floor tile needs replacing and I have one in the closet." A long-term goal: "I'd like to get a new couch for this room." Then, get started, room by room. But don't try to do everything at once. Take the first day to do as many of the short-term goals as you can, and you'll feel great.

208 repair list

Keep a list of things around the house that need to be fixed. As time passes, you may find that it's easier or cheaper to fix a bunch of things at once or that you won't need to fix certain things at all, things you haven't used in a while. Of course, you should get rid of those things immediately. On the other hand, some people believe that it's more organized to fix something at once or get rid of it. Your choice.

HOUSEHOLD CHORES

209 bring Mohammed to the mountain

Don't make a zillion trips around the house picking up waste baskets and bringing them outside. Instead, get a big plastic garbage bag and take *it* to the garbage, emptying all of the waste baskets into it on-site. Start in the room farthest from the outdoor garbage cans and work your way trash-by-trash through the house.

210 pail liners

There are two ways to avoid always having to run to the kitchen for a new garbage can liner. Keep a batch of liners in each room that has a can. If you want to be really organized about it, keep a few folded liners at the bottom of each can. When you throw away the garbage, a new liner will be ready and waiting. The other alternative is to use environmentally conscious reusable garbage bags for dry garbage. These are widely available in houseware stores and stores that specialize in organization, such as The Hold Everything Store and catalog.

211 double garbage cans

Double and triple garbage cans are great for separating wet garbage from dry garbage, glass from plastic, recyclable from nonrecyclable, or compost from trash. Organizing stores and catalogs offer a variety of options.

212 all-purpose

Try to minimize the number of different products you use, such as those you clean with. Not only is it easier to work when you don't have to keep switching tools and supplies, but you'll have fewer items to shop for and store.

213 sign on the dotted line

Before you accept delivery of something, be sure to open the box and check that you're getting what you ordered and that it at least appears to be in perfect working condition.

JOURNALS

214 party journal

If you entertain frequently and you're so inclined, keep a journal of your brunch, lunch, and dinner parties so you'll know what you served, your shopping list for particular menus, what you wore, who came, what they brought, and so on. This will keep you from serving the same things to those guests next time, and it's a nice memento, too.

215 create-a-journal

Predesigned journals are available for keeping records of just about anything: your favorite wines, birthdays, children's growth, wedding guests and gifts, high school events, and so on. These journals usually come with appropriate blanks for you to fill in. Even if you prefer to make your own journals and memory books from a

large three-ring binder with pockets, a see-through portfolio of acrylic pages, or a photo-album, take a look at
predesigned journals for organizing ideas.

216 after school

Bring a notebook when you go to a museum, or
attend a lecture. Also keep notes on interesting books
you read and unusual facts that come to your attention. Don't worry, you're not going to be tested. The
notes will simply help you focus your thoughts, learn
new things, and remember.

KEYS

217 key house

Keep a decorative bowl near the front door for house
keys and outgoing mail, or hang a door pocket, with
key hooks, on the back of the door for the same purpose. As soon as you enter your home, put your keys
in the bowl or on the hook. If you never put your
house keys anywhere else, you'll always know they're
either on you, in the door, or in their place. When you
leave, take the keys and the mail. An added bonus:
People who live with you will know at a glance
whether you're home or not.

218 the key to your keys

If you need to keep track of many different keys (and
who doesn't?), key tags can help you remember what
each key is for. One useful product is Helix's KeyTi-
di—a plastic wall-mountable key organizer with labels
and hooks for six keys. Mount it discreetly in a closet.
If security is an issue, mark your key tags with coded

labels, or purchase a small steel Fortress KeySafe, which comes with an index, twenty-five key tags, and twenty-five hooks on which to hang them. Both products are available at office product retailers.

219 extra key

If you haven't already done so, take the time to leave extra house keys with a trusted neighbor. Do *not* label them with your name and address. Ask your neighbor where they will be kept (somewhere safe, hidden, and out of the way). That way, you will know where they are, just in case your neighbor forgets or neglects to tell other family members.

220 extra car key

Keep an extra car key in your wallet, in a compartment intended for pictures or credit cards. If you lock you keys in the car, chances will be greatly improved that you won't be left out in the cold.

KITCHEN & FOOD

221 prepare to cook

Before you start cooking from a recipe, be sure to read the recipe all the way through. As you read, assemble the ingredients; you don't want to get to the middle and find you've forgotten something. Then take out all the pots, pans, cooking utensils, and serving dishes you'll need, and there's no way you'll be caught short.

222 kitchen timers

Don't give it a second thought: To avoid burning the food as well as the house, when you put food on the stove or in the oven set a loud timer. If you don't have a whistling tea kettle, do the same when you put on water to boil. Set the timer for a few minutes before the food is due to be done. This will give you time to take care of any last minute preparations, such as getting out a cooling rack or a potholder. If your food hasn't finished cooking, don't go away without setting the timer again!

223 grandma's stuffed cabbage

Keep a shopping list of ingredients for often-used recipes on file with the recipe so you don't have to make one up more than once. Check your cabinets before you go. Then pencil-check the items you'll need, specifying the amounts. Erase the pencil later so you can reuse the list.

224 platters that flatter

Somehow food tastes better when it's organized beautifully on a platter. Think about color and texture when you're planning a meal—particularly for guests. Try to include some variety. When serving several foods on one platter or plate, put contrasting colors and textures next to each other—white mashed potatoes next to bright green broccoli, for example. Choose pretty platters that will set off the meal.

225 spice of life

Put fresh spices in bottles with labels indicating what they are and the date. If you have a lot of bottles, alphabetize them on a spice rack the way you would store-bought spices. Keep those spices you use regularly near the cooking area, but store the excess in a cool, dark place. If you have the space, apply self-sticking Avery labels to the tops of the containers, and store them—alphabetically—in a shallow kitchen drawer.

226 padding

With a plan, and a few simple organizational tools, it *is* possible to lose weight. The most successful diet plans instruct dieters to write down everything they eat. Carry around a little pad with your pocket calorie-counter, and keep track of what and how much you eat during the day. That way, you'll know as soon as you've exceeded your limit. If you still don't lose weight, look back over your entries to determine where you may have gone wrong, and adjust accordingly.

227 refrigerator follies

If you're afraid to use something in your refrigerator or freezer because you don't know what it is or you're afraid it's too old, throw it out right now. Do not give it away, and by all means, do not leave it there. A month from now, it'll just be a month older.

228 once is enough

When you unpack your groceries, put all refrigerated items next to your refrigerator and open the door just once. You'll save time and electricity.

229 freezer use

Tape a freezer storage guide, telling you how long frozen foods keep, inside your pantry cabinet. If you have enough space in your freezer and you're making something that freezes well like spaghetti sauce, make a double batch and freeze one. Label what you freeze and include a "throw date." Do the same with food given to you by others, and include the source. Check your freezer from time to time and plan to use frozen foods before their throw dates.

230 eat in

Even if your kitchen is not quite big enough to be called an eat-in kitchen, it's possible that you could still sit and eat in it. Is there a free wall where you can fit a table top on a hinge that flips up and locks into place? Even if there's only room for a small table, you can use it for additional work space.

231 under sink

Use the space under your kitchen sink. Install wire sliding shelves on the sides. Put a Rubbermaid removable clean-up caddy behind the door. Just be careful that everything is positioned in such a way that the pipes won't get bumped and the shut-off valve is left unobstructed.

232 wine racks

Wine should be stored on its side so that the cork stays wet. So if you store wine, you need a wine rack. It supports the wine on its side while preventing the bottles from rolling into each other and breaking. Wine racks come in a variety of shapes, sizes, and prices to suit any decor and budget. Leave them visible if they complement the room. Otherwise keep them in a cupboard, closet, or in the wine cellar. Be sure to choose a cool storage spot protected from direct sunlight.

233 handy tray

Keep a kitchen tray handy by hanging it from hooks— on a wall, on the side of a cabinet, or from the bottom of a wall grid. You'll be surprised how often you'll use it once you remember it's there.

234 basket saver

One decorative and unusual way to keep your kitchen clutter-free is to hang things in baskets from the ceiling: teas, bananas, herbs, dried flowers, pot holders, bibs, etc. This method is especially effective if you have children.

235 Rubbermaid

If you are decorating, redecorating, or building a new kitchen, you can purchase cabinetry that comes with beautiful built-in features like garbage cans on the insides of doors and sliding shelves. But if you want to transform existing cabinets without much trouble or expense, Rubbermaid makes a large line of products that function the same way. One of the most useful is the pull-out drawer. It screws into the floor of the cabinet, and then the attached tray slides out, making low, high, and hard-to-reach cabinets much more accessible and easy to use.

236 speaking of Rubbermaid

Once you get their Wrap and Bag Organizer, you'll wonder how you ever survived without it. Sold in groups of three, it is a simple, inexpensive product that conveniently holds plastic wrap, aluminum foil, and garbage bags in an upright position. Get those long skinny boxes out of your drawers, where they're hard to get to and take up valuable kitchen storage space. Put them into the Wrap and Bag Organizer, which you can hang inside a cabinet door or on a discreet section of the kitchen wall or pantry.

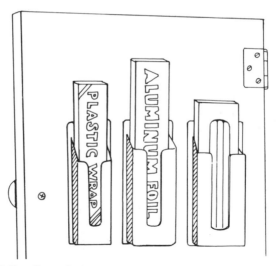

237 wash deco

Hang a pretty decorative hook on the wall above the kitchen and bathroom sinks to use for hanging your watch and any other jewelry you take off when you wash or do dishes. Place the hook in such a way that the jewelry will stay dry and won't be jostled or fall into the basin when you remove it.

238 double trouble

When you end up with two half-used containers of the same food (e.g. ketchup or spices), check that they have approximately the same throw dates, and then combine them.

239 knife for life

If you do a lot of cooking, it's important to have a complete set of knives. There are many useful knives designed for specialized tasks, but the following are basic to any well-equipped kitchen: a paring knife for paring and slicing fruits, vegetables, and other small foods; a utility knife for a variety of tasks; a chef's knife for chopping; a poultry knife for deboning and slicing chicken, turkey, and other meats; and a long, serrated bread knife. You will also need a knife sharpener, and it should be used regularly. There are many types of knife racks, but the one I find most useful is a wall hanger that holds the knives in place with magnets.

240 under cabinets

Keep your valuable kitchen counter space as clear as possible. Use the air space under high cabinets if you can. Attach hooks, brackets, and other special attachments, and hang cups, wine glasses, bread baskets, microwaves, and shelves. Sony makes an under-the-counter radio that includes a kitchen timer, clock, and cassette player. Once you start chopping vegetables to music, you'll wonder how you ever cooked without it.

241 wall grids

Kitchen walls should be more than just decorative. The things you use most often will be most accessible if they are hanging in plain view: paper towels, measuring cups, mugs, pots, utensils. Wall grid systems such as the one made by Heller are the very best for organizing your wall storage. They're quite attractive and they come in different colors to match your kitchen decor. You can add to the grid as your needs grow by purchasing special hooks, baskets, and even shelves.

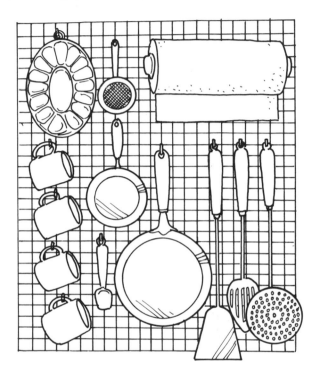

242 edible decorations

Keep flowers, seeds, rice, grains, sugar, and beans in see-through airtight labeled containers. Put those items that require dark storage in a cupboard.

243 cupboard wise

Relegate things you rarely use to the top of the kitchen cupboard and keep often-used items on the handiest shelves, which are usually at eye level. Keep things together that you use together, such as everything you need to prepare breakfast. Glasses are most handy placed right near the sink. Cooking pots, pans, and utensils should be near the stove. For easier storage and retrieval, keep pot lids all in one place, standing them on their sides and in size order. Either designate a deep drawer the "pot lid drawer," or get a pot lid organizer, available in houseware and organizing stores.

244 hang cups

Especially if your coffee cups won't stack, hang them from hooks on your cabinet ceilings. Even if your cups do stack, using air space is always a great idea.

LAUNDRY

245 mesh sorter

Separate your laundry into little mesh bags before you put it in the wash. These bags are often sold as lingerie bags, and many people use them only for that purpose. But these handy little items are also perfect for keeping track of different family member's socks, underwear, and other small items. Get a bunch of them. When the wash is done, just throw the bags in the dryer and these pesky little items will come out presorted.

246 sock lock
Safety-pin your socks together before doing the laundry.

247 takes all sorts
Don't wait until you're ready to do your laundry to sort it. When you undress, save a few steps by putting clothes directly into the proper laundry piles—hot-water whites, warm-water colors, and cold-water delicates and separates—or put clothesdirectly into mesh sorters. You can use several laundry baskets for this sorting if you have a lot of room, or you can buy a laundry basket with compartments at a bath or organizing store.

248 cold water only
Keep special washing instructions for clothes in a see-through portfolio file, and keep the file alongside your laundry detergent. Or pin them up on a corkboard near your washer.

249 linen bundles
Keep bed linen sets together for quick and easy bed-making. Fold and wrap top and bottom sheets and extra pillowcases together, place in a matching pillowcase, and store in the linen closet or a bedroom drawer.

250 ready to wear
When folding your laundry, fold complete sets of gym clothes together into little parcels. Put them into a drawer as a bundle or put them directly into your gym bag. Each parcel should include one of everything.

251 here's the hook

Hang a hook in your laundry room, in the front of your closet, or near where you do your ironing for holding just-ironed garments, and for holding shirts on hangers while you button them before putting them in the closet.

LISTS

252 on the run

Consider making verbal lists, especially when you're in a hurry. Get a small, portable voice-activated tape recorder and record your ideas, long- and short-term plans, and memos to yourself and others. You may also want to use the recorder to tape your interviews and business meetings. When you get home at night, transfer those notes onto paper and sort them into your files and lists.

253 every day

Whether you use a personal organizer, a pen and paper, computer scheduler, a hand-held computer or a Post-it pad, sit down every morning and take the time to plan your day. You'll accomplish much more that way than if you just let the day happen. In addition to scheduling appointments in your appointment book or calendar, generate a daily activity list.

254 remember the list

Before you go to sleep, start a list of the projects you plan to accomplish the next day. The more you plan the night before, the better prepared you'll be tomorrow. Go over your day's activity list to see that you did everything you wanted to do and called everyone you needed to call; carry over unfinished items to tomorrow's list. When you go to bed, leave the list and pen near your cereal box or on your kitchen table. That way, you'll be sure to see it and can add to it as you eat breakfast.

255 file card lists

File cards make good daily activity lists because they're compact, and sturdy and tuck right into your appointment calendar, serving as both a reminder and a bookmark. Use a ruler to subdivide a single card into categorical sections such as personal calls, work errands, personal errands, work calls, busywork, fun activities, letters to write, presents to buy, ongoing projects, decorating ideas, things I owe my sister, books to read, or whatever seems appropriate that day. Or divide your list into different cards and keep the most important ones on top. Personalize your list in a way that works for you. Cross off items when you complete them or change your mind about doing them.

256 activities advance goals

You need to decide what your goals are so that you can list and prioritize your activities. First, list your goals—immediate, upcoming, and long-term—and then list your activities. Group your activities according to your goals. Remember that your most important activities will advance your goals.

257 all right, already

Put undesirable but necessary tasks, such as cleaning out a closet, on your daily activity (to-do) list, and if you update your list before you've completed the task, carry it to the next list. It may take a while if you procrastinate, but eventually you'll do it—if only so you don't have to be reminded of the chore every day.

258 your ABC's

Whether you're at work or at home, whether you're the boss or the mailroom clerk, it's important to set priorities early each day, but be flexible enough to change your priorities when something more important arises. Assign your most important tasks an *A*, your next most important tasks a *B*, and so on. Something that's a *B* one day can easily become an *A* the next. In fact, that's what ought to happen. The filing, for example, can build up for only so long. Eventually it has to be done.

259 first things first

Prioritize your daily activities by listing them all and then numbering them in the order in which you intend to do them. If you want to be a good time manager, take care of the important things first rather than the easy things. Many busy people procrastinate by always attending to unimportant details. Then they end up frazzled and puzzled when, at the end of the day, they don't have time or energy for the important things.

260 the red flag

Still another way to prioritize your daily list of things to do is to color-code your activities. Write your most important tasks in a bright color such as red, or after listing all of your daily plans, use a yellow or green highlighting pen to draw your attention to top-priority tasks. If you use a highlighting pen in an appointment book, be sure the color doesn't bleed through onto another day's activities on the reverse side of the page.

261 satisfaction guaranteed

If your list is on a plain pad that you plan to dispose of after you've accomplished everything, cross off tasks after you've completed them. If your list is kept in your yearly diary, appointment calendar, or personal organizer, check the items as you complete them. There's hardly anything more rewarding than crossing or checking off all the items on a list and having time left over.

262 reward yourself

Offer yourself real rewards for completing tasks as planned. If you finish all the top-priority items on your list within a certain period of time, allow yourself to participate in a fun leisure activity, or schedule a nap for yourself, or a relaxing dinner in a restaurant, or an hour with a friend.

263 consistent shortcuts

Over time, try to be consistent about how you refer to items on your list. If possible, abbreviate frequently repeated items. Assorted items that go under a larger general category should begin with a short acronym for the category, such as *MTG* for "plan meeting," followed by the type or name of the meeting to be planned.

264 magnetic pads

The best place to keep a memo pad is on the refrigerator. Some companies manufacture particularly useful pads with magnets on the back. They're better than erasable memo boards for last-minute shopping lists because you can rip off the top sheet and take it with you when you're on the run.

265 fast notes

Many of the things we put on paper we need for only a very short time, and then the paper gets tossed. Post-it pads, lists, journals, and personal organizers— they're all great, but for short-term notes, these methods waste paper, need updating, and take up space. For quickie notes, nothing beats Vertiflex's Erase-a-note. It sits on your desk at a comfortable angle and should be used for temporary reminders, short and immediate "to-do" lists, one-time phone numbers, and meaningless doodles. The magnetized pen sits right on it for easy access, and there's a small well for holding papers and envelopes. After you transfer important notes to a more permanent location, use the special eraser to wipe the pad clean with a couple of effortless "magic" swipes. No more paper waste or desk mess.

266 fun lists

Lists help make the most of your leisure time as well as organize your chores and work. Keep a fun list with you at all times. On it, put recommended restaurants, movies, videos to rent, books to read, and compact discs, records and tapes to buy. When you've seen the movie or read the book, cross it off your list. After you've eaten at the restaurant, transfer the address to your address book if you liked it, or cross it out if you didn't.

MAIL

267 lap desk

If you're like me and you need a desk but don't like to sit at one, get a lap desk. They come in beautiful woods, but if you want something lighter, eldon/Rubbermaid makes one out of sturdy plastic with lots of compartments. Inside you can keep your letterhead, envelopes, pens, stamps, return address stamper, bills that need paying, and letters that need answering. Take it to the couch, flop down, cross your legs, and get busy!

268 mail station

Set up a mail station at home. Spin-rite makes an item called a Personal Message Center that is perfect for this purpose, but the stationery store is filled with similar organizers if you find one that is more suited to your needs. I like the Personal Message Center because the tabs that separate the sections stick up and are still readable after the mail is inserted. And, it holds a lot. Assign each section a useful heading such as "bills to pay soon," "mail," "letters to answer," "upcoming events," "mailing offers," "recipes," and "calls to return." Make sure each section is something you are sure to use, and no matter what, be sure to make the last section, "miscellaneous."

269 mail call

Never let your mail sit around. Read your mail as soon as it arrives and sort each envelope into the following categories: pay, answer, file, or dump. Then do it. Be selective about what you choose to file; think about whether you'll ever need to locate that paper again, and if you do, will you really be able to find it? Your time is too valuable to spend constantly filing; and your home shouldn't resemble the archives of the Library of Congress.

270 to be considered

If you receive a lot of mail that you don't have time to completely absorb or attend to but that requires you to make a decision eventually, keep it all in one file. Call the file, "to be considered." In that file, put mailings about magazines and journals that you're thinking about subscribing to, events that you may or may not attend, sales that you may or may not take advantage of, and credit offers that you may or may not accept. Keep each mailing in its envelope, and on the outside of each envelope, mark the expiration date of the offer or the date of the event or sale. Check your file frequently, and dispose of any expired mailings and those that you are finally able to make a decision about. If a particular mailing appeals to you, pencil a note on your calendar or in your appointment book on the appropriate day or days.

271 all stamped up and no place to go

Set out a hundred envelopes and a roll of 100 stamps. Put stamps on all the envelopes, and if they aren't preprinted with your name and address, have a return-address stamper made, and stamp them. Do this one day while you're talking on the phone or watching television. When your supply gets low, do it again. Be sure to have some extra stamps of higher denominations and some blank envelopes on hand, too, for heavier mail.

272 hi! lite

Use a highlighting pen when you read letters to note important items, a change of address, or something you want to follow up on. You will save time when you transfer information to other sources, such as your address book, or when you answer the letter. You may also want to attach Post-its to the letter (if you don't want to write on the letter itself) to help you remember how you want to respond.

273 voice mail

When your hands are busy but your mind isn't, such as when you're doing dishes or knitting something simple, use the time to write personal voice letters on a portable voice-activated tape recorder. You'll get twice as much done. Also, a voice letter is a personal and fun form of communication, and for every letter you "write" during borrowed time, that's one less letter you'll have to write by hand.

MEMORY

274 where is that thing?

Think for a minute. Are there certain things you waste a lot of time looking for over and over? If so, you probably need to assign each one a permanent place, and learn to keep it there.

275 door sign

If you're afraid of forgetting something important when you leave the house, put a sign up behind the door. You may want to remember to shut off the lights, take out the garbage, take your keys, shut off the heat or air conditioner, and so on. If the problem isn't remembering what you have to do but remembering at all, hang something such as a shopping bag around the doorknob you'll be using when you exit.

276 daily reminders

Attach a large clasp to the inside of your front door. If you want to remember to do something like deposit a check or buy an essential toiletry, clip a note to the door. That way, you can't avoid seeing it when you leave.

277 daily reminders II

A wax erasable board with an attachable pen serves the same purpose as a magnetic clasp and it's neater, but the drawback is you can't take the notes with you. Choose the wax board reminder method, however, if you keep a daily list with you at all times and simply want extra insurance that you'll remember important things.

278 morning reminder

If you want to remember to do something first thing in the morning, such as cancel a doctor's appointment or make a phone call, and you're afraid you'll forget, leave a Post-it note on your bathroom sink. You'll be sure to stumble into it the next morning, even if you're still half asleep.

279 memory tripper

Place anything you want to take with you when you go out, such a package to be mailed or laundry going to the cleaners, right in front of the door so you would literally trip over it before you'd forget it. Of course, you should make sure no one else trips over it.

280 shower power

If you're in the shower and think of something you want to do as soon as you get out, and you're afraid you'll forget, put the shampoo on the floor of the tub, over the drain. You'll almost surely notice it as you get out, and it should remind you of what you wanted to remember.

281 the right combination

Always forgetting your lock combination? Get a lock that allows you to set the combination yourself. Then make up a combination that you won't forget. Use a relative's birthday or a best friend's phone number or your bank code (if you know it by heart). When setting your own codes and combinations, it's usually not a good idea to use your own birthday if security is an issue because that's the first code someone else would think to try.

282 forget me not

Don't rely on your memory especially if you tend to forget things or have a busy schedule. Make a deal with yourself that you'll never make an appointment without writing it down in your appointment book. This may sound compulsive, but you won't be sorry.

283 where is it?

Do you have trouble remembering where you put important papers or jewelry or the keys to your safe deposit box? Create a file in your computer called "Where is it?" Every time you put something away that you do not intend to use frequently, record its location in your computer file. Use a password if you want the file to be confidential. If you don't have a computer, you can use your filing cabinet.

MISCELLANEOUS

284 umbrella saver

There's always a risk of losing your umbrella when you put it down in the bank, for example, or hang it on a countertop near a store's cash register as you reach for your wallet. True, you do need to free up your hands, but there are several alternatives to putting down your umbrella:
1. Use a big umbrella with a strap that hangs over your shoulder.
2. Use a small umbrella that fits in a tote bag over your

shoulder or a mini one that fits into your pocket.

3. Hang an umbrella with a hooked handle on your belt, or coat pocket (if the fabric isn't delicate).

4. Bring along a two-foot rope or ribbon, tie the ends, hang it over your shoulder and hang the umbrella from the loop.

285 double exposure

Always have extra film on hand for your camera. As soon as you take your last picture on a roll remove the film to be developed, pop it into the empty canister from the new roll, and load the new roll into the camera. Label the canister with the date and contents, if you don't like surprises.

286 new suit

If you think you're involved in an incident that may lead to a lawsuit or formal complaint, take notes while details are fresh in your head. Include dates, times, people's full names, conversations and everything else you can think of.

287 foyer

If you don't have a formal entrance hall or foyer, create one near the front entrance to your home. A foyer should have a little table for putting down things like gloves and hats; a mirror for quick fixes upon entering or leaving; a small rug, tub, or mat for wet shoes; an umbrella stand; and a coat rack if there isn't lots of room in the hall closet.

288 door hook

Attach a sturdy hook to the *outside* of your front door for temporarily hanging bags, dry cleaning, and other bulky items while you get out your keys.

MONEY

289 first things first

To avoid losing track of the checks you write, always enter the check information in your check register *before* you write the check.

290 month by month

As accountants will tell you, it's a good habit to start a new ledger or check register page at the end of every month and to begin a new check register at the end of the calendar or fiscal year. This makes it easier to research old payments and to avoid duplicate payments, and to prepare taxes.

291 pen check

Keep a pen tucked into your checkbook register, marking the current day's entries. Also, keep your bank card, deposit slips, and a calculator with your checkbook. While other people are filling out their forms at the counter, you can get right in line. While you wait your turn, use your pen to write checks, fill out deposit slips, and make entries in your check register. When you get to the front of the line, you'll be ready.

292 no-slip bank slips

Many people find that when they withdraw money from banking machines, it's often inconvenient to make an entry in their checkbook; consequently, they lose track of their balances and bounce checks. But there's an easy remedy: When you use an automated teller machine to withdraw money or make a deposit, always take the receipt and tuck it into your wallet. Make a deal with yourself that you'll never remove your receipts from your wallet without entering them into your checkbook.

293 reconciliation

Balance your checkbook as soon as your statement arrives each month; that is, make sure your records and balance agree with the bank's. If you don't know how to reconcile your checkbook, see the back of your monthly statement for a simple, straightforward formula. Your reconciliation is sure to work out if you and the bank have kept a careful record of all your transactions. An adding machine that prints a record is not essential for this task, but it is extremely helpful.

294 paid

After you've paid a bill, date it and mark it "paid" or "pd." Also note the check number. Then transfer the bill from your "bills-to-pay" file to your monthly "paid-bills" file, or to one of your "taxes" files, or to the file for the individual account.

295 credit control

To control credit spending, keep a separate check register with each credit card. You can set your "balance" at your monthly budget or at your credit limit. Each time you use the card to make a purchase, write down the information in the check register as if you were using a check, and deduct the amount from your balance. When your balance is at or near zero, leave the card and the register at home. After you've paid your monthly bill, reset the "balance."

296 receipt drawer

Every time you get a credit card receipt, put it in the same temporary file or little drawer. Keep the month's receipts together until the bill arrives. Then check the receipts against the bill. If there are any discrepancies, call the credit company, but first check the expense against your appointment calendar; you may have forgotten you were at a craft fair on the day of the mysterious charge.

297 bill-paying station

Whether you use an extra napkin holder, a box, or a silver toast tray, it helps to have a single bill-paying station. Put all bills there as soon as you receive them. Keep the station supplied with a return address stamper or labels, postage stamps, a calculator, a pen, and anything else you typically use when you pay bills.

298 interesting

Don't wait until bills are overdue to write the checks; on the other hand, don't pay them too early and lose bank interest on your money. Here's my method: Prepare all bills for sending at the soonest convenient time. Write the checks, prepare the envelopes with return addresses and stamps, and enclose remittance forms (and file your copy); do everything but seal the envelope. Next to the glue on the envelope, write the due date in shorthand (12/31 for December 31, for example). Keep the bills ready to mail in the order you want to mail them, and check the group before you leave the house in the morning. Then just seal and mail.

299 spend thrift

When you're budgeting, don't just consider the cost of an item you're thinking about buying. Consider the related costs as well. For example, if you're buying a suit, think of the expense of dry cleaning. If it's a car you want to buy, you must also be able to afford gas, maintenance, insurance, tolls, and more.

300 saving strategies

Whether you're saving just to have a nest egg or in order to make a large purchase, one of the best ways to save money is to deduct a fixed amount from each paycheck. Decide how much of your income you can afford to live on comfortably, and save the rest. Put your savings into accounts that earn high interest while allowing you to withdraw money as necessary.

If possible, it's usually wise to put as much as is allowed by law into tax-deferred retirement accounts such as Keoghs, 401K's, IRAs, and other company-sponsored plans.

301 the early bird gets the work

In most situations, it's good to be early, but here is one where it's worth waiting. Many credit card companies offer year-end summaries that are almost indispensable for complicated tax preparation. If possible, don't finalize your taxes until you've received your year-end summaries. The summary also provides a great record of your spending habits and helps you to forecast, plan, and budget for the next year.

302 the seven-year ditch

With the exception of certain specialized forms (8606 regarding IRAs; 2119 regarding sale of homes; 8582 regarding passive-activity-loss limitations; and 942 regarding paying taxes and insurance on behalf of household employees), it's generally OK to throw out tax records that are more than six years old. If you're uncertain, call the IRS help line and ask.

303 the three *C's*

When you're figuring out your expenses for tax purposes, be sure to look carefully in the following three places: (1) your checkbooks and bank statements; (2) your credit card summaries; and (3) your cash receipts or petty cash book, if you have one. In most cases, that should cover it! Your expense books and contemporaneous diary should corroborate. You shouldn't have to go riffling through hundreds of individual pieces of paper to figure out how much you spent during the year.

304 tax files

Divide your tax files into the categories you know you use or into the categories that your credit card company uses to summarize your expenses: entertainment (leisure, restaurants); travel (car rental, hotel/lodging, transportation); merchandise (gasoline/automotive, household, mail order, retail stores); health care (medical services, prescriptions/supplies); education; and miscellaneous.

305 basic but essential

If you itemize your taxes, get into the habit of asking for receipts for everything. Because you may not always be thinking about taxes, if you don't make it a habit you won't get many of the deductions you would be entitled to for items for which you pay cash. Also, receipts are good for returns, warranties, and proofs of purchase. Decide later if the receipt represents a deductible item.

306 tax trick

Keep your tax-deductible receipts together in one place until you are ready to analyze and file them. Think of such receipts as money. That's what they're worth to you. Regardless of whether their ultimate destination is a single file (i.e., a messy heap) or a neatly categorized filing cabinet, make a deal with yourself never to file a deductible receipt until you have entered the amount in you tax record under its appropriate heading. After you've entered a receipt in the book or on the screen, make a little check mark on the receipt itself to indicate that it was entered, and then file it. This can be done daily, weekly, or monthly. If you wait until the end of the year, you'll have a big job ahead of you.

307 back to business

If you plan to deduct a meal that you have charged on your credit card, you'll have to document it as an entertainment expense. Before you tuck your credit card receipts into your wallet, write down on the back who you dined with and the nature of your business. The backs of most credit card receipts provide a place for noting this information.

308 donations

When donating clothing and other items to charity, don't just dump your donations into a brown bag. You may be entitled to a tax deduction. Make two copies of a list showing each item and its condition. Print your name, address, and date on the list. Many charities will validate your list with a signature or a stamp, keep a copy, and return one to you. You will not only have the good feeling of helping people and a record of where your old coat went but, very possibly, a useful tax document. The IRS prints guidelines to using donations as tax deductions; get them and keep them with your tax forms.

309 safe keeping

If you worry about your valuables at home, get a safe deposit box at a bank. Keep a list at home of what's in the safe and, if necessary, have the items insured. Keep any available proof of ownership with your list. Good things to keep in a safe are deeds; stocks and bonds; passports; birth, death, marriage certificates; and expensive jewelry and small heirlooms. Leave a copy of your will in the safe, but not the original, which should be kept secure but accessible at home or with your lawyer or executor. Don't assume that the contents of your safe are covered under your homeowner's policy or the bank's insurance policy; if you haven't made special arrangements, chances are they're not insured. Better check.

310 hiding spots

A good place to hide some emergency cash and your safe deposit key at home may be in a pet food box on a high shelf in your kitchen pantry, but only if you can be sure that there's no risk that you or someone else will throw it out. This works best when you're in charge of feeding the pet or when you have no pet. Advise other family members. Another good hiding spot for small or flat valuables and a little cash is in an envelope taped securely to the back of an inexpensive wall-hanging. Here's hoping that burglars don't read organizing books.

311 photo record

Nobody wants to think about it, but...use a Camcorder or camera to document what's in your home in case of fire or burglary. And don't just rely on the pictures. Doubly protect yourself by making a list of your assets and keeping it in a file labeled "assets" or in your "insurance" file. Keep with the list all available documentation of value and ownership; receipts and appraisals, especially for major assets, are especially helpful when you're making insurance claims. Keep the list in a fireproof safe or safe deposit box. Likewise, take pictures of what's in your safe deposit box, and keep them safely at home.

312 credit check

One way to keep track of your credit history as well as to be prepared in case of loss or theft is to photocopy the credit cards and other items in your wallet or purse. It's easier than making a list. If you photocopy the backs as well, you should have most of the phone numbers you would need to call in case of loss or theft. Keep the list in a safe, secure place, such as a fireproof safe or filing cabinet, with other important documents such as deeds, birth certificates, and so on.

313 waist belt

Especially when traveling or shopping, use a waist belt or hip pack instead of a pocketbook or shoulder bag for storage. Keep your money safe, your hands free, and your shoulders comfortable.

314 credit card insurance

If you have a lot of credit cards, consider registering them with a company that will cancel them all if they're lost or stolen. That way, you only make one call.

315 sdrawkcab

If you need to carry around numbers such as automatic teller machine passwords, phone card numbers, bank account numbers, social security numbers, and other private numbers that are difficult to memorize, list them backward. Put dashes in the expected places so that they won't look backward to a pickpocket. Your social security number 123-45-6789, for example, would read 987-65-4321. Reduce the list on a photocopy machine several times, and cut it to fit in your wallet. To make the list sturdy and permanent, back it with cardboard and cover with clear wrapping tape. Keep it in your wallet behind a credit card or photo.

316 on a roll

Don't wait until your den looks like Fort Knox to ask the bank teller for empty coin rolls. Banks will provide these free. Sorting change is a task that many children enjoy—especially if they're allowed to search out the old coins to add to their collection. Disposable or washable work gloves are recommended for this unsanitary task, and children should be told not to touch their faces when handling money and to wash when they're through.

317 be precise

It's not a good idea to double the tax in a restaurant in order to figure the tip because frequently the tax is wrong and the tax varies from place to place. Fifteen to twenty percent is the recommended tip for waiters and waitresses. Bring a small calculator with you when you eat out. Multiply the amount before tax by .15 or .20 to calculate a fifteen or twenty percent tip.

318 loan sharp

If you're shopping for a mortgage or loan, it's important to research and prepare. There are many books that explain how bankers use your income, savings, and assets to determine whether you qualify for a loan. Study the newspaper over the course of several weeks, if possible, to learn what rates are currently being advertised. Ask the banks to tell you what their special loan requirements are. Figure out whether you are likely to qualify for the loan *before* you ask the banker whether you qualify, so you can anticipate questions and objections and prepare your answers in advance.

319 borrower or a lender be

When you borrow or lend money, books, CDs, or anything else, keep track of it in a log, and keep it with your cash. Encourage the other person to do the same to avoid misunderstandings later. Note when the money is to be paid back or the item is to be returned. Your appointment book can be used for this purpose as well.

320 gamblers beware

Don't go to a casino without a budget and a plan. Know how much you are willing to lose, and take only that amount of money with you. If you're on a gambling holiday, divide your total gambling budget by the number of times you plan to enter the casino, and take only one portion with you at a time. In addition, decide in advance how much you would need to win before it would be worth it to you to stop gambling. Resist the temptation to spend more than your limit; leave credit cards and checks behind. If you happen to win your goal amount before you lose, leave the casino and don't go back.

MOVING

321 room to move

Most stationery stores sell self-stick colored dots that are great for moving. When you're packing to move, color-code your boxes. For example, put a yellow dot on all the boxes that you want the movers to leave in the master bedroom and a blue dot on all of the boxes to go in the kitchen. Get to your new place ahead of the movers, and stick the appropriate dot in the doorway of each room so they'll know where the first boxes go. Most movers like this system.

322 box bonanza

If you're moving, go to a liquor store. They have sturdy boxes that are ideal for packing books and other small, heavy items. They even have bottle separator inserts that will divide and protect your glassware and other valuables. Liquor store boxes are far less likely to have bugs in them than supermarket boxes, and liquor store owners are usually delighted to let you take their boxes away, no purchase required. By the way, you don't have to be moving to take advantage of this free resource. Think of the liquor store when you're mailing lots of gifts during holiday time or looking for a storage box.

323 box step

When you're deciding which pieces of furniture will work in your new home, consider not only color and style but size. Take careful measurements of your furniture, and if you're not artistic, make box figures that show the measurements. It's easier to visualize an item in a space when you have a visual representation and not just the measurements. Bring your "artwork" to your future home, and make notes about where each item will go. If you find something won't fit, the measurements will help you describe the item in your garage sale advertisement.

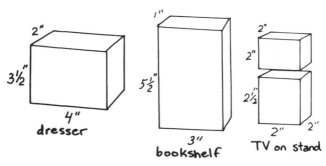

dresser

bookshelf

TV on stand

324 how do I get there?

Instead of spending several awkward minutes on the phone every time somebody asks you for directions to your new home, be ready for the question. Prepare directions to your new home from north, east, south, and west. Draw a little map beneath your directions, or use a local map. Make several photocopies, and when people plan to visit for the first time, send them one. Or send them out with your change-of-address announcements. Always have a few copies on hand. They will remain useful until you move again.

OFFICE & BUSINESS

325 home office

For efficiency as well as potential tax deductibility, a proper home office requires a separate designated area. Whether your home office takes up a whole room or part of a room, keep in it everything you need to run your business—desk, stationery, files, and so on—and try to confine your work and your supplies to that area.

326 stamp rolls

Buy rolls of stamps instead of panels. They're much quicker to work with and easier to store.

327 mail checklist

Your mailing station should include many or all of the following: postage of assorted denominations, wrapping paper and tape, boxes and envelopes in assorted sizes, mailing labels, a typewriter, forms for different types of mail (registered, certified, express, UPS, Federal Express, etc.), a current list of postal charges (available from the post office), tape, a stapler, jiffy bags, a postage meter (if you send large quantities of mail), some preaddressed labels to people you send frequent mailings, the phone number of the post office, a zip code chart or directory, pens and markers, a wet sponge, a staple remover, and assorted stampers with such messages as "handle with care," "first class," and "priority mail."

328 post office alternative

Mail Boxes Etc. USA, with outlets nationwide, provides an excellent alternative to waiting in line at a busy post office—particularly during holiday time. They charge more than the post office for packing materials and postage, but they'll pack your boxes for you if you like. Remember, your time is worth money, too. Unless minimizing cost is essential, go to Mail Boxes Etc. instead of the post office whenever it is more convenient and can save time. If you use them frequently, you can even open an account.

329 be a team

For your own sake as well as your company's, don't try to do everything yourself. Delegate tasks whenever possible. That's what management is all about.

330 may I take a message?

If you find that you waste a lot of time talking to people you don't need to talk to or being interrupted during important matters, it's probably a good idea to hire someone to answer your phones for you and screen your calls. Moreover, your phone time is spent much more efficiently when *you* do the calling (because you're prepared) and when you return all your calls in a single block of time.

331 all in one

Portable desk-accessory kits that come complete with tape, pencil sharpeners, pencils, scissors, tape measure, ruler, pen, stapler and staple remover, and other such office necessities are useful if you attend conventions frequently or plan a lot of meetings. But adapt the kit to suit your individual needs. Kits are not the best choice for general office use. For your desk, carefully select the full-size accessories that best meet your particular needs.

332 Port-a-Pocket

If you attend a lot of meetings, ask your office supplier for a clever little item called a Port-a-Pocket. It's a portable, expandable, see-through vinyl hot file that hangs with velcro on a wall or door. Put your meeting notes in it, a pen, a calculator, floppy disks, papers, forms, files, and other small supplies. Keep it on the wall or divider in front of your desk, and grab it when you leave for the meeting. At the meeting, slide handouts into the Port-a-Pocket where they'll stay visible, and if there's no table, the Port-a-Pocket will double as a lap desk. If you need to, you can insert documents into it, and instead of marking them up write on the vinyl with most inks; later wipe it off with a damp cloth.

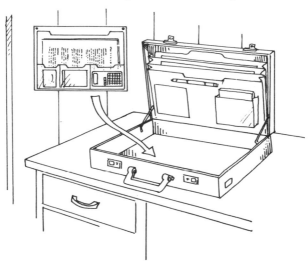

333 name tag strategy

If you're responsible for planning a meeting that requires attendees to pay in advance, prepare the name tags for each attendee as you process the payment. If you don't have a premade name tag for someone who arrives at the meeting, you'll know that he or she hasn't paid. If RSVP-ing is required but not payment, prepare the name tags when the RSVP is received. Either way, count the tags to see how many people are expected, and arrange them in alphabetical order for easy distribution.

334 the road to success

Success Notes by Columbian Art Works, available through your office supply dealer, is an invaluable tool for meeting-goers. At first glance, it looks like an invitingly designed notebook, but, in fact, it's much more. In addition to special features that allow you to organize your notes on each topic, draw diagrams neatly, and flip quickly to particular material, it introduces an organizational system that I highly recommend. The system is simple: For every note you take, add a quick circled code in the margin indicating whether the item is (F) to be Followed up on, (A) something to Act on, (I) an Idea, or (R) Reference information to file later. The "FAIR" system allows you to process your notes easily after the meeting.

335 separation of home and work

Designate a single place in your home for everything that needs to come to work, and likewise at work, designate a place for things that you need to take home.

336 take breaks

You're not a machine, and even machines need rest. Get out of the office. Go out to lunch or go shopping or take a walk around the block. Clear your mind and move your body. A person can't be productive from morning until night without at least one good breather.

337 clear it out

If not at the end of every day, then at least by Friday, you should be able to see the bottom of your in-box. At work and at home, make this your mantra: Read it, do it, file it, or dump it.

338 closing up

Just to be sure you don't forget anything when you leave your office, tape a list of locking-up procedures to the back of the front door. The list might say, "Turn off air conditioning; turn off computer; turn on answering machine; lock both locks." A list is especially important when the last one out is not always the same person.

339 batch jobs

If you know you're going to need to call for several messengers or send several faxes or mail several letters over the course of a day, don't mail, fax, send, or stamp one letter at a time. Set up a regular time toward the end of the day when you will prepare all outgoing packages or correspondence, with the exception of emergency messages. Batch mailing jobs, but don't wait so long that the mail won't be delivered on time.

340 make room

When you receive an assignment that's going to generate a lot of paperwork, immediately clear an unobtrusive space for it—on a shelf, in a drawer, or in your filing cabinet—and clearly label the space.

341 changing times

Norman Schreiber, author of *Your Home Office* (Harper & Row), advises, "When you set up your office, remember that you'll probably change it as you business changes. Make sure that all objects are movable, and all areas are accessible." Great organizing idea.

342 ergonomics

When setting up your daily work space, make everything adjustable. From the lighting, to the height of the chair, to the tilt of the computer monitor, you should be able to change everything with ease. Think of your back, your eyes, your neck, and your general comfort.

You'll work better, longer, and healthier if you aren't locked into one position—much less one uncomfortable position.

343 inventory check

It's a hassle to run out of supplies such as staples, paper clips, letterhead, and printer ribbons. Set up an inventory sheet and use it to do a monthly inventory check. Don't wait until you've run out of something to reorder it. Your sheet should list all of your supplies, the date each was last ordered, and the quantities and amounts ordered. That way, you can track how long supplies tend to last and adjust future orders accordingly.

344 custom desk

Custom build your own file-storage desk using two two-drawer filing cabinets topped with a large painted or polished wooden or formica board cut to order at a lumber yard.

345 every inch of space

A typical desktop contains the following: pens, pencils, paper clips, rubber bands, postage stamps, envelopes, floppy disks, memo pads, Post-it notes, a small calculator, a ruler, a letter opener, push pins, scissors, and other assorted paraphernalia. Most of these items should be sorted into individual areas and kept accessible. Go to an office supply store and choose the desktop organizer and drawer organizers that will work best in your space.

346 money matters

Most office supply stores are filled with ledger paper and ledger books for keeping track of all money matters. If you deal with money—even if it's just the petty cash box—buy a basic accounting book and learn a few bookkeeping tricks. Particularly useful is learning how to post debits, credits, and running balances, and how to read and deal with statements, invoices, financial reports, and bank records.

347 office grids

Wall grids have come out of the kitchen and into the office! Whatever the room, the best place to keep things handy but out of the way is on the wall. Rather than make a kitchen unit suit your office needs, ask your office supplier for a Vertiflex wall grid. It's specifically designed for office use and comes with all you need to mount it on the wall or hang it over a partition. It comes with two letter trays, a hanging folder holder, and two different kinds of file racks.

348 look it up

Keep a ready reference library on your desk: a good dictionary, thesaurus, almanac, desk reference, and style and grammar book.

349 bulletin on bulletins

No room for a bulletin board? Not inclined to have a messy board dominate your wall? The solution is simple. Get a Spectrum Diversified Designs Memo Strip or a Davson Bulletin Bar II. Working on the same principle as bulletin boards, these are minibulletin strips that allow you to tack up notes discreetly just about anywhere, even on windows! They attach with magnets or self-adhesive tape and will prove useful in most rooms of the house, at the office, in a locker, and even in the car.

350 vertical hot files

Most desks need a multiple-file desktop organizer for holding and dividing current projects into separate vertical hot files. They come in a variety of sizes, shapes, and materials and are made by such companies as Vertiflex, Safeco, Delco, HiPro, and Buddy Products. When a file is no longer active or "hot," pare it down, throw it out, or move it to a permanent file cabinet in order to make room for new hot files.

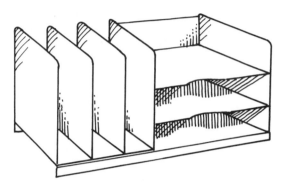

351 stackable trays

Stackable letter trays are great for separating paper and stationery, envelopes and labels, and other desktop items. They work well as in- and out-boxes, too.

352 last one first

When you're photocopying a batch of sheets one sheet at a time on a machine that produces the copies face up with the first on the bottom and the last on the top, turn your stack of originals over, so they're face down, and photocopy the last page first and the first page last. Your copies can then be removed from the copier in order! Be sure to keep the originals face up as you finish with them or you'll have to reorder them.

353 desk necessities

Without getting up from your desk, you should be able to reach your hot file containing today's or this week's projects, pens, pencils, sharpener, paper, calendar, scissors, tape, Post-its, paper clips, letter opener, stapler, staple remover, telephone, telephone directory, and trash basket. You should also have instant access to any other equipment you use frequently, such as a typewriter, computer, or calculator.

354 estimating a job

If you are an independent contractor, look at any available material on a project or one like it before you estimate how long it will take and what it will require of you. Keep careful time sheets for when you need to estimate similar jobs in the future. Set your fees in advance, allowing a cushion for miscalculations. Whenever possible, procure a contract. Visualize the entire job before beginning. Clear up any questions as soon as they arise, preferably before starting. Assemble tools before beginning. Don't jump in until you know what is required of you.

355 money due

If you perform services that require you to bill people, or if you're expecting several refunds or payments, it pays to have at least a rudimentary invoicing system. In a folder or a series of folders arranged by due date (a tickler file), keep copies of invoices, requests for refunds, and individual notes to yourself describing who owes you what, what you did for them, how much they owe you, and when payment is expected. Put notations on your calendar reminding you to request each payment if it hasn't been received on the due date. When a payment arrives, remove the invoice from the folder, mark it "paid," and file it.

356 save a tree

Instead of throwing them out, recycle your bad photocopies. Use the backs; they're still good for writing notes, sending faxes, and other purposes. Turn used paper over and toss into a very handy box labeled "scrap." The next time any piece of paper will do, take a piece out of the box.

PARENTING

357 maternity dressing

Think ahead when shopping for maternity clothes. Buy clothes that can be worn throughout your pregnancy and, if possible, afterward so you have the largest possible wardrobe for the longest time. Avoid elastic waists and tight knits that look roomier than they are. Select skirts and pants with adaptable or built-in maternity stretch panels, and cover them with very big, long T-shirts or sweaters.

358 beep, beep, it's a girl

Never let it be said that hospitals don't change with the times. Many offer a new technological service. They rent beepers to expectant fathers. When the mother-to-be goes into labor, the father can be notified quickly wherever he might be. Depending on you situation, if your hospital doesn't rent them, you may want to consider buying a beeper. It can be useful in any emergency.

359 cluster tasks

If you have children and can't get out of the house whenever the mood strikes you, it's important to be organized about your outdoor activities and tasks. Plan you outing well and not haphazardly. If you plan to have lunch with a friend, see if you can leave enough time to stop at the library, pick up boots for the children at the shoe store, stop at the drugstore, and still have time to pick the kids up from school.

360 soap dispensers

For people with infants and small children, the Dispenser by Better Living Products, Inc., a wall dispenser for soaps, lotions, and shampoos, is an "indispensable" organizer for bathrooms and nurseries. Convenient and easy to use, it keeps your hands free, eliminates plastic bottle clutter, and is neat and attractive on the wall. Now you can dispense the baby lotion quickly with one hand while holding the baby with the other. Buy lotions and soaps in bulk. It is far more economical and better for the environment than buying lots of individual disposable bottles and jars. The Dispenser, available in houseware and organizing stores and catalogs such as Hold Everything, comes in a variety of sizes and is designed for home use. It comes with everything you need to install it safely anywhere.

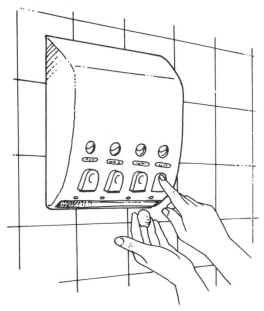

361 baby beep

There are some things you can't afford to forget. Wear a beeper watch to remind you when it's time for baby feedings, baths, doctor visits, and anything else you don't want to have to think about all the time.

362 lunchtime

Organizing expert and parent Elaine Martin Petrowski recommends turning your bread box or bread drawer into a lunch station. In it put sandwich bags, twist ties, paper bags, bread, granola bars, lunch or milk tickets, and all the other items that you use every day to make you children's lunches. Keep the lunch boxes in or near the drawer, too. In the morning or the night before, set up your materials in an assembly line and pack them right up. Get the kids to help.

363 never too young

Teach children how to organize by making it an activity they'll enjoy. If children were taught how to file, they wouldn't grow up to be adults who drown in paperwork. Get your children brightly colored file crates, file folders, and labels. Help them set up files they'll want to use, such as rock star facts and photos; friends' birthday data; a party journal; maps; music sheets; creative writing and poetry; and pen pal correspondence.

364 lost and found

Children are always losing things. You can't expect them to be as organized as you are. Label all their clothing—especially those things they're likely to take off (eyeglass cases, book bags, gloves, hats, etc.). Forgetful adults might consider initiating this practice for themselves as well.

365 quick fix

Keep a checklist for the baby-sitter on an erasable wax board that allows you to update it easily. Right before the sitter arrives add new care instructions for the children as well as where you can be reached. Emergency instructions and a list of where to find things will most likely remain unchanged, so keep those instructions posted on the board. Hang the board in the kitchen, and keep it just for this purpose. If there's too much information to keep on the board, use a notebook, and keep the notebook in a kitchen drawer.

366 storage cubes

Square storage cubes placed on their sides and stacked are very organizational and attractive in children's rooms. They hold toys, books, clothes, and anything else you can think of.

367 toy boxes

Don't improvise here. Select toy boxes that are designed to be toy boxes, and double-check that they conform to stringent safety standards: Toy boxes should have air holes, lightweight lids, and plastic hinges, and they shouldn't lock.

368 crayorganization

It's never too early to learn good habits, and being organized and neat is a good habit. Crayola has a line of art organizers for holding crayons and other art supplies. Among the more interesting items are a caddy filled with "washable" art supplies, a revolving crayon carousel, and a draw 'n' do desk. The desk itself is meant to be colored on with the assorted art supplies that are housed neatly within it, and then wiped clean. These supplies help children learn that good organization can enhance creativity rather than hamper it.

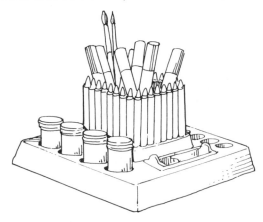

369 ClassCases

ClassCases, available in two sizes and in lots of bright colors, are inexpensive, lightweight colorful briefcases for kids. They hold and organize art supplies, school supplies, Barbie Doll clothes, blocks, other toys, or food for picnics. High dividers keep the contents in place when transported. The lids snap off so they can be used for drawer organization as well. Parents will want to steal these cases for first-aid materials, travel, cosmetics, sewing, fishing tackle, jewelry, nuts and bolts, and their own drawers, but get your own instead. ClassCase has designed a case for teenagers and adults. They call it the "cosmetics and travel case." It has all of the above features, and it comes with an unbreakable acrylic mirror.

370 cooking with crafts

Parents, try to enlist your children to help you in the kitchen in a way that keeps them occupied and teaches them at the same time. But for those times when it doesn't work, keep a scrap paper and crayons in a kitchen drawer for ad hoc arts-and-crafts projects while you're cooking.

371 they'll grow into it

Two-purpose items that grow and change with your child, such as a potty that becomes a step stool or a changing table that becomes a dresser top, help keep your home clutter-free and functional.

372 deco-kid

Especially while your child is young, select furniture and other items that match the decor you worked so hard to achieve. If your home is modern, look for a high-tech high chair. If your home has a country flavor, pile toys into straw baskets and antique wicker chests. An added bonus: You'll want to keep many of these items long after your child outgrows the toys.

373 look up

Just because you have children doesn't mean you can't keep your things accessible and your home beautiful. Just look up. Choose hanging plants instead of floor plants, and mobiles instead of statues for decorating. Put things in baskets that hang from the ceiling and high on secure wall shelves.

374 for posterity

Don't think you have to keep all the drawings your children make and all the reports they write, but don't throw out your children's creations without their approval. Instead, start a practice that will keep your home clutter-free while teaching your children organization and sensible decision-making. Teach them to be selective about what is saved. At the end of every semester, decide together which few things are worth saving for posterity. At the end of every school year, help them reevaluate the choices made in prior years, and if appropriate, pare down the collection.

375 quality time

It's very important to spend quality time with your children every day, that is, time spent doing something mutually enjoyable. If the time doesn't just occur, it's important to plan for it. Take a walk together, cook a meal, visit a friend, or ride bicycles. If the only way you'll make time is to schedule it, then schedule it, and assign it a high priority.

376 locker power

These days, many companies, such as ClassCase, Class Act, Deflect-o, and Dek, make products that are designed for locker organization. Your older children will appreciate them. They'll be able to add shelves, pockets, mirrors, and compartments to tall, skinny steel lockers that typically contain only one shelf. And it's worth it because your children use their lockers several times every day, and for better or worse, it's theirs for the whole school year. Many of the products can be used at home, too. For example, the Doorpouch by ClassCase is magnetized, and so it works just as well on refrigerators and file doors as it does in lockers.

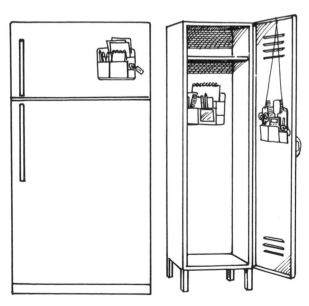

377 kid lists

If you swear by your lists, notebooks, or personal organizer, perhaps you'd like to teach your children to use these tools. Your system, however, probably won't appeal to your children, no doubt being too complicated and colorless. You'll be glad to hear that you can get personal organizers for children of all ages. Day Runner makes an adorable Dinky Diary Organizer for grade-school children complete with a pen, calendar, cartoons, stickers, diary, and a place to keep track of friends and birthday parties and presents. Get a Student Time Planner by Class Act for your teenagers.

READING, RÉSUMÉS, & REPORTS

378 adjustable bookshelves

The best bookshelves are adjustable. Books come in all different sizes, and adjustable shelves not only allow you to use space efficiently but are capable of storing very large or oversized books upright.

379 color coding books

If you have a large library, color-code your book spines with Avery labels. Colors might stand for fiction vs. nonfiction, mysteries vs. romances, autobiographies vs. biographies—whatever helps you find a book quickly. If it isn't obvious to you what the colors stand for when you're done, tape your color-coding system to the inside cover of the first book on the shelf, or tape your list to the underside of a shelf (incidentally, this is a good hiding spot for cash and certain valuables). If your books are divided by section, be sure to leave room for growth in each section.

380 extra paper

Many books have blank pages at the end. Use these pages to make notes about what you've read, doodle, sketch, or make lists. No reason to let perfectly good paper go to waste!

381 book ID

Get a stamp or stickers that say "This book belongs to *Your Name*" or "From the library of *Your Name*." This is especially helpful if you tend to lend books out and want them back. If you keep an inventory list of your books, mark down the loan on the list, or just make a note in your appointment calendar of who has it and the date you expect the book back. You shouldn't have to call the person, but it may be your only chance to see your book again. On the other hand, if the book's not a collectors's item and you never intend to read or refer to it again, don't let it clutter your life. Give it away. Someone out there will enjoy it.

382 don't let them pile up

Be sure to dispose of last month's magazines before the new ones arrive. If possible, instead of tossing them, pass them along. Ask family, friends, and neighbors if they would like to receive particular magazines on a regular basis when you're through. Get rid of clutter and make people happy at the same time.

383 magazine-reading management

Have a plan when you read a magazine or newspaper, and keep Post-it pads and retractable blades with you at all times. If you're not giving the magazine or paper away, either read the articles at once or use a retractable blade to cut articles out to read later. If you don't want to destroy the magazine or paper—perhaps you plan to give it away—use the Post-its to mark the pages you wish to read later. You may also wish to mark articles that you want to recommend to others, or you may wish to note sales, classified ads, and so on. The point is to be sure the next time you pick up the magazine or paper—if ever—you don't have to read the whole thing to get to the items you want.

384 magazine storage

Many manufacturers make magazine holders for bookshelves, and these are great, but do yourself a favor and keep only extraordinary issues to which you expect to refer frequently. The magazine holders I prefer are transparent so that you can read the titles on the spines and are colored to blend with the decor of a room.

385 that's it

If you find that the magazines from one of your subscriptions pile up and rarely or never get read, cancel that subscription.

386 reading basket

Washington, D.C.-based writer Linda Stern cleverly advises, "Keep a reading basket equipped with stapler, scissors, and highlighter pen, and use it to store all the magazines and newspapers you want to browse through. You can carry the basket around the house with you; when you get time, sit in your favorite chair, go through the basket, clip and staple what you want, and toss the rest."

387 résumé help

Peggy Schmidt, author of *The 90 Minute Résumé* (Petersons, 1990, 1992), advises that the best way to organize a résumé is to set up a series of worksheets. Label each at the top: (1) personal; (2) work (your titles, dates, and places of work); (3) education (degrees, dates, and names of schools); and (4) extracurricular activities. Put each on a different page, and brainstorm a sketchy list. Aim to create a bare-bones outline; don't try to write down everything.

Then give these outlines to another person who will help you by simulating an interview; your "interviewer" will ask you questions based on your outline, and your answers will help you develop and refine your résumé. For a better idea of how this works, consult Schmidt's book.

388 drafts

To maintain control of multiple drafts of reports, résumés, presentations, or manuscripts, use paper of a different color for each stage of the project, such as yellow for a first draft, pink for a second draft, and so on. Don't make too many photocopies of a work in progress. Keep your eye on all the copies. Recycle the backs of old versions by clipping off a small corner, turning them face down, and putting them in a box marked "scrap."

389 yes, master

If you have circulated more than one copy of your most current version of a report, résumé, presentation, or manuscript in progress, label one copy "master." This is the only copy on which you should make changes. If anyone writes suggestions on other copies that you want to incorporate, transfer them to your master. If you create a new master, mark the old one "foul."

390 plan a speech

Know your subject and main point. Keep focused. Create an outline that has a beginning, a few clear points you need to expand and illustrate one at a time, and a conclusion. If possible, start your speech with a light or humorous anecdote, or ask an intriguing or trick question. It's helpful when the main body of your speech has a clear and easy-to-remember framework, such as who, what, where, when, and why, or a problem, then a solution. Determine how long your speech should be in advance, and keep to that length. Know who your audience is so that you can design your speech to reach the majority of listeners.

391 write a speech

Create an outline of your speech only (see above) rather than the whole text to encourage you to speak your speech rather than read it. A good outline is essential to good organization. With a speech, an outline is doubly important because that's all there is. Double- or triple-space the outline text onto large index cards, and don't justify the margins, so that you can find your spot very quickly if you look up.

392 practice a speech

Get a tape recorder and sit in front of a mirror. Use a clock or watch with a second hand to time your speech. Check the clock, hit the start button on the tape, and go. Practice looking into the mirror rather than at your notes. Do this several times until you're confident, comfortable, and satisfied.

393 deliver a speech

The outline of your speech should be typed on very large index cards so that you don't have to shuffle a lot of unwieldy pages. Use your finger to mark the line or section that you're up to. So that you will project your voice and remember to look up, address your speech to someone in the last row.

394 job search

If you lose your job, don't panic, and don't act out of desperation. Develop a plan before jumping into a job search. It's especially important to exercise, eat nutritiously, sleep enough, and stay positive and healthy. What exactly do you want to do now? Bring your résumé up to date, and circulate it with a plan, or think about whether the time is right to start your own business. Either way, this is where the networking and note-taking you've done will pay off. If you've been lax in that regard, improve now. Remember, you're far more likely to find work through networking than from classified ads. Always follow up job interviews with a polite and intelligent letter of thanks.

395 on hand

Don't get caught in a bank line, supermarket line, or movie line or on a bus or train without something to read. Carry a book, newspaper, magazine, or clippings with you at all times.

SHOPPING

396 follow up

When you order a product through the mail, tear out the page from the catalog, and staple it to a piece of paper containing all ordering information, such as reference numbers, the company's name and address, how you paid, the amount, the day's date, and the date when the product is due. Put it in a file called "mail-order follow-up," and make an entry in your appointment calendar on a day by which the product should have been received. When the product arrives, go directly to the follow-up file and check it against ordering information, and then toss the papers or file them. Mark the item "received" in your appointment calendar.

397 catalog collector

If you like to order from mail-order catalogs and you enjoy keeping them, keep only the most current ones. Use a separate magazine holder for them, and keep them alphabetically within it on a book shelf. When the most current catalog arrives, if not sooner, throw out the prior one.

398 coupon clipping

As long as you haven't collected a truckload of coupons, arrange them by their expiration dates. (If you do have a truckload, you'll probably have to organize them first by product type.) Make a file that separates the coupons by month and keep the ones that are about to expire in the front and the ones that never expire in the very back. When you clip coupons, circle the expiration date; at the end of a month, throw out any expired coupons and move the file divider to the back, right in front of the coupons that never expire.

399 coupon clipper

If you have a truckload of coupons because you always clip them and very rarely use them, stop clipping right now, and give away or throw out the ones you have! Chances are they've all expired anyway. The next time you're tempted to reach for the scissors, think of all the time you wasted clipping the batch you threw out.

400 supersmart

Find out what day of the week your favorite supermarket puts out its sale flyer, and plan to buy the paper that day. Note how long sales are good for and plan to shop before the sale is over. Now, play the "match game." See if you have manufacturer's coupons for the items on sale that week. Make up specific shopping lists of what to buy, but also pay attention to varieties, amounts, sizes, brands, and whether you have a coupon or not. Don't buy things you don't tend to use no matter what the savings.

401 superdupersmart

If you use a lot of coupons, it's worth your effort to locate a supermarket that doubles the savings, even if you have to go a little farther to get to it (assuming the prices aren't much higher than at you local supermarket). If you're really dedicated to cutting costs, play the match game at more than one supermarket, and note the final cost of each item so that you can purchase it at the least expensive store.

402 coupon keeper

The Conimar Corporation has thought of everything when it comes to food shopping with coupons. They manufacture the Magnetic Coupon Keeper & Shopping List Envelopes. These are pads of envelopes that attach with a magnet to your refrigerator. Each envelope has lots of lines on one side for your shopping list, and a checklist on the back of the envelope allows you to keep track of your coupons. The coupons, of course, go inside the envelope! If you can't find this product at your local discount store or elsewhere, take their lead and write your shopping list on envelopes, keeping the coupons inside, and ticking off the items for which you have coupons.

403 spend and save and spend

It can be fun to keep track of how much you save from clipping coupons. Before you go shopping, list the coupons you plan to use, including their value. When you get home, check off the coupons you have used. Add those up and keep a running record in a pocket shopping notebook. At the end of every month, deposit a percentage of your savings in the bank, and treat yourself to something special with the rest!

404 rolodiscount

Keep a Rolodex card or cards under *D* for "discount." List all the discount numbers available to you: travel discounts, shopping-club numbers, annual sale information, and so on. Include any membership numbers or sale codes you need to give to activate the discounts.

405 armed to shop

Use a pen, Post-its, and scissors or a retractable blade when reading supermarket ads and catalogs. After you've marked or torn out everything that interests you, throw out the rest. Take the ads with you when you go shopping, and then throw them out, too.

406 know when the sales are

There are few things more infuriating than buying something expensive and seeing it on sale the next day. Most stores put particular items on sale at regular and planned intervals. It pays to keep track of when certain stores have big sales or when certain items tend to be on sale everywhere. Ask at the stores if you don't know. If you use a personal organizer, create a page called "shopping" for sale information. Or keep a file at home.

407 good consumer

When you're shopping for an expensive item, shop around. Keep a notebook of the different models you find, as well as their features. Cut out ads from newspapers. Find out the best prices and ask about delivery charges, warranties, and hidden costs, too. Learn what questions to ask. Unless you're very knowledgeable about the item, avoid salespeople and shops that don't encourage you to ask questions.

408 holiday shopping for children

If you want to be prepared, take less time, avoid crowds, keep your sanity, and spend less, start your Christmas and Hanukkah shopping for children months ahead of time. Consider the growth factor when buying clothes. Toy store sales are worth hunting out! While you're in line waiting to pay or while you're at the cash register, make a list of what you're buying and for whom; hide the gifts and keep the list on you at all times.

409 personalized food-shopping list

Take a pad and pen to the supermarket. Starting at the end furthest from the frozen foods, go down aisle after aisle writing down all the products you tend to buy frequently, including preferred sizes, until you've covered every aisle. Take the list home and redo it so it's very neat. Add a few blank lines after each section and at the end. Photocopy it several times. This is now your shopping list. Use it yourself and distribute it to other members of your family who do the food shopping. Make sure they understand your shopping route so they can use the list most effectively and efficiently when they get to the supermarket. Save the original, and make new copies before you run out. Or write your original list on a reusable memo board, check off what you need, and wipe clean just the check marks.

410 clutter equals disorganization

Don't acquire anything unless you know its purpose in advance. Even if you know the purpose, reexamine the need. Then think about the price; then think about the placement or what storage space it will require. Still want it? Ok, go ahead and buy it.

411 bring the cards

When shopping for lots of gifts, such as at holiday time, prepare greeting cards at home before you shop. Put the recipient's address and your return address on each envelope and then take them with you so that you don't need to bring your address book to the store. Enclose the cards with the gifts before having the clerk wrap them, and, if possible, have the store mail them for you.

412 dress smart, not rich

When you're going out for some serious shopping, arm yourself by wearing loose, light comfortable clothing. Wear sneakers. Take an empty canvas shoulder bag. Wear a belt bag instead of carrying a pocketbook. Leave your expensive jewelry at home. If you look too wealthy, you'll be a target for pickpockets and thieves.

413 buy for later

When you're in a card shop and see a funny get well

card or a clever new baby card that you're sure you'll use one day, buy it. If you find the perfect card for a particular friend but her birthday is months away, buy it, and make a notation in your appointment book reminding you that you have a card, and reminding you to mail it a week ahead. Keep the cards filed with your gift wrap and ribbon or in your desk grouped in the same categories as at the card store: anniversaries, birthdays, and so on. Don't go overboard. You don't want to keep the cards so long the paper browns.

414never run out

You don't want to wait until you're out of something you use regularly to buy more. If you do, you'll not only be inconvenienced but you'll probably end up paying too much. (Ever buy suntan lotion at a beach drugstore or film at Disneyworld?) Always have at least one extra on hand of items you use regularly (toothpaste, toilet paper, contact lens solution, etc.); moreover, make a note to buy more when you see that you're getting low. That way, you'll never run out.

415big purchase

When you're considering purchasing something large, ask yourself where you're going to keep it. Measure the area and take your measurements with you when you shop. Measure the doorway, too, to be sure you can get the item into your home.

416reuse bags

If you're concerned about the environment and feel guilty throwing out shopping bags but have no place to store a lot of them, get yourself a big straw bag or a tote bag. Take it with you when you go shopping, and ask the checkout people to use your bag instead of theirs. If you do end up bringing home some bags, reuse them as garbage bags or take *them* with you next time you go shopping.

417 eat something

As you finalize your food shopping list, have a meal or a snack. If you're hungry in the supermarket, you're more likely to overspend, buy things you wouldn't buy otherwise, or eat too much when you get home.

418 written estimates

If it's a major expense, whether for an item or a service, always try to get a written and signed price or estimate. Then shop around.

SPECIAL OCCASIONS

419 social register

An excellent way to remember birthdays, anniversaries, and other important occasions from year to year is with Success's *Social Register*, available in many office supply stores and discount department stores (or call 1-800-888-8488 for the Success dealer nearest you). This elegantly designed record book provides a perennial calendar for listing yearly events and introduces a system for organizing your gift giving and card sending. In the back of the book are pages for listing up to fifty personal profiles (your best friend likes cats; your boss's favorite color is blue; your mother-in-law always wanted a gold locket; etc). These profiles can be cross-referenced through a simple record-coding system with the front of the book. The book also allows you to keep track of the gifts and cards you send and receive to ensure that you won't send someone the same gift year after year, or heaven forbid, give people back the gifts they gave you! Use the book as it suits you. You can use just the event record in the front or just the personal profile record in the back. You can use the book to keep track of business acquaintances only or family only. Whatever works; it's your book.

420 holiday gift list

Start your holiday thinking way before you start your holiday shopping—with no stress to the budget. During the year, if a particular gift strikes you as suitable for someone, make a note of it and put it in a holiday-gift-list file. Or if someone lets you know of something she or he wants, put a note in the file. Depending on the length of your list, the time of year, and your shopping habits, you can keep the list with you in your wallet or leave it at home. If you do buy a gift for someone, make a note on your list.

421 year after year

Occasions that you want to remember from year to year should be listed on a single page in the front or back of your appointment calendar. Rather than repeating all the information each year, number every event on your list and write the same number on the date of the event in your calendar. Circle it in red or another bright color, or draw a party hat around it so it will grab your attention. At the end of the year, transfer the information to the next year's calendar. Make notes in your calendar before certain events to send cards and gifts so that they will be received on time.

STORAGE

422 use all the space

The best arrangement for a closet will allow you to see all or most of the contents, with the most frequently used items within easy reach. You don't want to have to move a lot of things to get something out, and you don't want to touch even one other thing to get a frequently used item. As a rule, the only things that should be stacked are things that are virtually identical, such as towels of the same size.

423 undershelf storage basket

Keep the distance between shelves minimal, while allowing for all items to fit comfortably. If you have extra space, use undershelf storage baskets. One of my favorites is a wire shelf that self-attaches with no screws, hammers, or clamps. It simply slides onto the next shelf up. These are made by Lee/Rowan, Heller, and other manufacturers of white wire organizing products. They are sold in home stores, organizing stores, closet stores, and department stores.

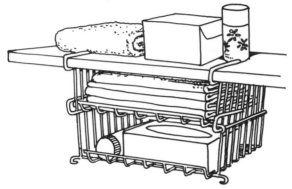

424 pro storage

For great ideas on how to revamp your closet, visit a closet or organizing store. You can buy closet systems and individual pieces that will help you get the job done yourself, or the professionals there will design your new closet for you. Many will even provide installation as a separate service. Or look through the classifieds for professional closet specialists. Some specialists will work with the contents of your closet as is, and others are more aggressive and will literally come over and tell you what to get rid of. Still others are essentially carpenters, who will build a new closet for you. As usual, your needs and budget will dictate.

425 closet light

Particularly in big closets, it's good to have a closet light. If you like, buy one at a hardware or houseware store that turns on when you open the closet door and goes off when you shut it.

426 closet hooks

Put sturdy hooks that hang over closet doors without tools and hardware on every closet door that doesn't already have a shelf, hook, or rack. Use the hooks for hanging shopping carts, bags, pocketbooks, ironing boards, and other hard-to-store or bulky items.

427 drawer organizers

For maximum neatness, each drawer should be divided into compartments. If you can't find organizers in just the sizes you need, get adjustable organizers that can be cut to fit.

428 window seats

Built-in window seats are the best thing for small rooms since murphy beds. They're attractive and comfortable and provide lots of hidden storage space in the cabinets beneath.

429 under stairs

If space is an issue, don't let all that beautiful space under stairs go to waste. Build or buy shelves to fit.

430 cabinets à la mode

If your bathroom and kitchen cabinets don't go all the way to the ceiling, or the top of your refrigerator is bare, you can place things on top of them such as decorative baskets, but remember that anything up there is likely to get dirty quickly and may be inconvenient to keep clean. If you want to use the space better and prevent dust and dirt buildup, have small cabinets built to fit.

431 in-wall storage

In-wall storage is, in a pun, neat. Think about recessing drawers, seats with hidden storage, and filing cabinets. Choose a suitable spot. Then have a carpenter cut out and remove a section of the wall, frame the opening, and insert the cabinet. The carpenter should be able to tell you if the wall you've chosen is suited to the task, and needless to say, careful measuring is vital.

432 fold-up wall desk

There's a product called a Desk Buddy that could prove very useful in cramped quarters where a writing desk is needed at a moment's notice. It works like a pullman bed in that it attaches to the wall, and when you pull it down, voilà! you have a desk with storage room for keeping pencils, a stapler, stationery, and other desk supplies. Made of industrial-looking metal, it's not too attractive, but in the right setting it could become indispensable—for example, in a small studio apartment, or a garage, laundry room, or attic that doubles as a wood shop or occasional "office" for yourself, an accountant, or a contractor. You can also attach it to the inside of a heavy closet door where it's out of sight and keep a folding chair inside the closet. Open the door, pull out the chair, and you have an instant office. You can order the Desk Buddy by writing to K-B-M Midwest Distributing, P.O. Box 734, Belton, MO 64012, or call 1-816-322-1615.

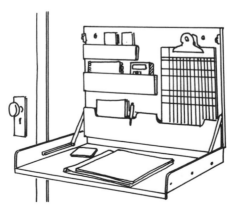

433 see and retrieve

Compartments are wonderful, provided items in the compartments can be recognized at a glance. You should either be able to see what's in each compartment or know what's in it because there's a clear label. This goes for desks, clothes closets, shoe boxes, cube storage, and filing cabinets. Neatness is only half the organization battle. Organization isn't worth much when you still have to waste a lot of time fishing for what you need.

434 measure

Regardless of what you intend to store or display, to make the best use of space list everything you want to provide room for, and measure the items and the available space with a tape measure. This will allow you to design your space in a realistic way.

435 small but roomy

To make large storage areas more manageable and to keep them neater, break them down into smaller compartments. Small things require only a small space, and that's the best place for them. Store everything in its smallest *comfortable* holder. Everything is better organized in a space that fits its size and shape.

436 prime space

Examine your home to locate and pinpoint prime storage space. Which areas are easy to get to? Which areas are hard to reach? Only often-needed items should go in prime spots. Infrequently needed items should take up the less prime spots. Get rid of never-needed items.

437 here, there, and everywhere

If you regularly use hand cream, Scotch tape, scissors,

aspirin, or anything else but in no particular room of your home, keep one in each room that you tend to use it in. You shouldn't always have to run all over the house to get something you use frequently.

438 halfway out the door

If you have a few things that you're not sure you want to get rid of, put them in a box or a bag for one month. If in that time you are never once tempted to use them or even wonder where they are or "miss" them, get rid of them.

439 a what?

If your toolbox or kitchen drawer is filled with alien thingamabobs and doohickeys for which you haven't a clue as to the purpose and can't conceive of one, it's time to be reasonable and dispose of them. Chances are if you ever need such an unusual item, it will be supplied with something else (e.g. a hook for hanging a particular mirror). Think about it: If you were told you needed a one-inch-square winch, would you even look in you kitchen drawer? No, you'd go to your local hardware or houseware store and ask for one. If you don't recognize it in your drawer, you won't be able to find it when you need it. So, good-bye.

440 hi, mess

Make friends with your mess—you shouldn't hate to open a drawer or a closet. Make a giant organizing task manageable by dividing it up into a series of smaller tasks, and don't expect too much from yourself. Set a time limit in which you expect to accomplish some portion of your goal. See it as a positive experience designed to make your life a little better.

441 don't deck the halls

Once-a-year things such as holiday decorations, Christ-

mas ornaments, Hanukkah candles, Easter egg decorating kits, New Year's Eve decorations, and noise-
makers should not take up prime storage space!
Gather these things together and make separate
marked boxes for each holiday. Store these boxes in
the same area (the "once-a-year" area), which should
be accessible but out of the way. See-through Rubbermaid storage boxes are great for creating long-term,
accessible storage.

442 crystal toadstools

Get rid of old gifts you never liked. Find someone who
loves them, or give them to charity. Your storage
space is too valuable to be cluttered with things you
never intend to display.

443 label all boxes

Every time something goes into a box, it should be
labeled as if you were moving. Be as specific as possible on your labels.

444 Action Packers

Rubbermaid makes a line of medium to large heavy-
duty storage boxes called Action Packers that I can't
recommend enough for long-term or outdoor storage.
They're handsome, double-walled, durable, well craft-
ed, and weatherproof. They can be padlocked and left
on the deck, in the yard, in a closet, in the basement
or attic, or anywhere else. Some are big enough to
hold golf and other sports equipment. You can take
them camping, fishing, boating, or to the beach.
They're great for keeping soda cold on a picnic. Store
your winter clothes in them during the summer and
your summer clothes in them during the winter.
Action Packers are sold at houseware and discount
department stores.

445 luggage storage

If you don't travel frequently, store large items in your luggage instead of in cardboard boxes, or store small luggage inside large luggage. Use removable masking tape to label the contents.

TIME

446 first this commercial message

Advertisers may not like me for saying this, but I'm going to say it anyway. Before you sit down to watch TV, plan to use commercial time. Take your sewing with you to your easy chair, or stretch your legs and wash some dishes. Pay a few bills or read the newspaper.

447 tick, tick, tick

Coordinate your estimates of how long something will take with your appointment book and your daily activity list. If you estimate that it will take a half hour to return all your morning phone calls and that will leave you with an hour free before your lunch meeting, look at your daily activity list and see what you can most efficiently accomplish during that hour.

448 if it's Tuesday, it must be laundry

One good way to organize your time is to schedule routine tasks for the same time each day or week, but be careful not to make your life too regimented. Leave yourself some unscheduled time every day.

449 easy as pie

Make a pie chart to represent how you spend your typical day. What percentage of your time is spent at

each task? How much time is left over for miscellaneous tasks? How much free time is left over for relax-
ation? Is this an efficient, worthwhile, productive
allocation of your time? Adjust as necessary.

450 time is money

Don't spend a dollar when you can spend a dime, but
don't spend a dollar to save a dime. Determine and
consider the value of your own time when considering
the cost of a project. Hire others, preferably professionals, such as tax preparers, housekeepers, and
mechanics, to do jobs that can be done more efficiently, more effectively, and less expensively by them
than by you.

451 don't just stand there

Do something! If you're waiting for the water to boil,
wash a couple of dishes or empty the dishwasher. If
your boss asks you to wait a moment until she gets off
the phone, reread your report or make a note about
your meeting.

452 odd hours

If you don't want to wait in line or get stuck in traffic,
try to avoid doing activities at times when the whole
world tends to do them. If you can help it, don't go to
the bank during rush hours, at lunchtime, on Friday,
or the day before a holiday. Try to go out to lunch a
half hour before or after the general population. Go to
the movies during the week or early on weekends.
Commute to and from work an hour before or after
rush hour. Ask your dentist and doctor when they are
least likely to be busy, and make your appointments
at those times.

453 speaking of doctors

Don't waste time in waiting rooms when you visit your
doctor, dentist, or other professionals who may not val-

ue your time as much as their own. Carry a paperback book, notepaper, and a pen for list making or brainstorming, or, better yet, a bunch of magazine and newspaper clippings that you have been wanting to read.

454 be efficient

Don't walk from Point A to Point B without taking something that goes there. Take items only halfway if that's as far as you're going. For example, if you're downstairs and need to take something upstairs, put the item at the bottom of the stairs, where you'll see it later, and take it with you when you go upstairs.

455 time savers

Whenever you can do so without making clutter, batch your chores. For example, don't write one letter at a time; wait until you have three to write. Don't type one label; again, wait until you have a few to type. If you have a page to photocopy, are not in a hurry, and expect to photocopy more later, wait.

456 take charge

To escape from time-wasting committee meetings, volunteer to take responsibility for solving a problem under discussion, even if you don't know how to solve the problem at that time. It may be obvious only to you that nobody else has a solution either and that a lot of time is being wasted in fruitless talk. Then go home and figure out how to solve the problem.

457 getting enough sleep

Figure out how many hours you need to sleep nightly and still function optimally. Estimate the longest amount of time it takes you to fall asleep. Add the two together, and subtract it on a clock from the time you need to wake up. That's your goal bedtime.

458 avoid oversleeping

Set a minimum of two alarm clocks—preferably one with a battery and one electric (that way, a power failure or a battery failure won't keep you from waking up). If there's a risk that you'll shut them both off in your sleep, place them across the room so you'll have to get up to turn them off.

459 rub-a-tick-tick

Put a clock in the bathroom; you'll be more likely to keep track of time in the morning and avoid being late.

460 the night before

Another good way to save time in the morning is to do as much as you can the night before. Make sure the dishes are washed and the garbage is out. Prepare tomorrow's lunch. Select tomorrow's wardrobe. Assemble what you'll need to take with you to work or school. Wash your hair at night instead of in the morning.

TOOLS & WORKROOM

461 can't be too careful

Children or no children, never throw sharp tools haphazardly into your toolbox. Before you store razor blades, saws, and knives, put them in a protective sheath, or tape the sharp edges with heavy wrapping tape. Leave nothing to chance. Sharp objects should be stored in such a way that they are most easily removed by the handle. If they are stored inside a box, the box should be labeled in large letters with the contents and *"CAUTION."*

462 tool systems

If you have a serious shop or hobby that just won't be contained in a toolbox, take a look at Rubbermaid's Work Space Tool Organization System. The system can be customized and grows to suit your expanding needs. The basic unit is a strip that can be mounted directly onto the wall or hung on a pegboard on the wall. Then units can be added, including utility shelves, parts drawers, wall pockets for such cumbersome items as saw blades, double and single hooks, clip hooks for holding paper and sandpaper, a screwdriver rack, a wrench rack, pegboard hooks and adapters, and a drill bit index. Mix and match. The Velcro company makes a tool storage system, too, as do other companies. Choose a system that's readily available so you can add to it. Regardless of what you choose, these systems will make you feel like a pro and your tool shop, room, closet, or shed will never be a mess again.

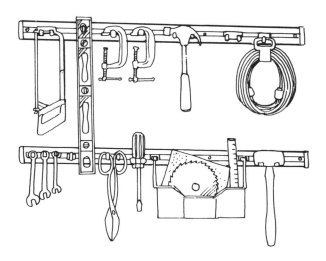

463 workroom wall grids

Wall grids may have been invented for the kitchen, but they work great in the workroom as well. Hang tools instead of spoons, buckets instead of pots, saw blades instead of food processor blades, trays of nails instead of spices. Consider your needs, resources, and space; then let your imagination take over.

464 shape up your shop

Keep your tools on a pegboard or hanging on the wall, and outline each tool's shape with paint or permanent marker. This will do a lot to ensure that they will end up back where they belong. Who could resist putting tools away in a shop like that?

TOOLS OF THE ORGANIZER

465 pocket tricks

One of the best tools to keep with you when you're not at home is a Swiss army knife or a minitool set. These sets should be complete with accessories you use often, or could need at a moment's notice or in an emergency, or otherwise have trouble putting your hands on quickly: a scissor, a nail file, a tiny screwdriver for loose eyeglass frames (these can also be purchased separately in supermarkets and hardware stores), a toothpick, a corkscrew, a paring knife, tweezers, and a can and bottle opener.

466 Post-its

Post-its aren't for everyone, but if they're for you, they're really for you. You can use them in many ways. Leave yourself messages on your phone; stick them on papers to be filed; mark articles you want to read in magazines; leave your spouse a note on the refrigerator; leave yourself a note on the front door. The uses are endless as your imagination.

467 Tacky Tape

Tacky Tape, an automatic dispenser that rolls out a layer of removable but secure adhesive, turns an ordinary piece of paper, an article, a recipe, a clipping, ribbon, a note, and so on into a Post-it.

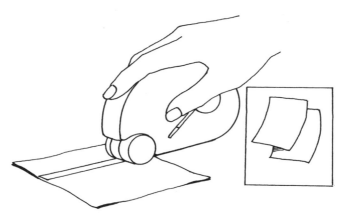

468 highlighting

Don't be caught without a yellow or green highlighting pen. Not only is it useful for studying, but it comes in handy when you read books, magazines, newspapers, clippings—anything that you may want to return to without having to read through again. Use it to highlight important items on your daily activity list.

469 click into place

Save time and energy wherever you can. Choose pens that click open and closed with one hand rather than ones that require you to remove the cap, store it on the end, and replace it later.

470 other tools

Throughout this book you'll find all kinds of uses for the following very basic organizational tools:

1. a plastic label machine for identifying boxes, file cabinets, and shelves
2. color-coded stickers for identifying cartons when moving and books on a shelf
3. files for keeping every piece of paper where you can find it readily
4. a retractable knife for neatly tearing out articles to read from newspapers and magazines
5. all-purpose hooks for hanging things on the wall, shelves, and doors
6. a tape measure for measuring items and storage space
7. pens and pads for making lists and taking notes

TRAVEL

471 read up

Whether you're traveling for business or pleasure, before you go to a new place, read about it. Know where you're going before you go so you won't have to waste time orienting yourself when you get there. Collect guidebooks, maps, and transportation information. If you have enough time, contact the chamber of commerce for each destination and request that they send you materials. If you'll be going to many different destinations, create a file for each.

472 short-lived information

Get all you can out of your guidebooks. Write in them; tear them up. They're rarely good for more than one or two years. If you're not going to use them again, ask the hotel clerk if they'd like to keep them for others to use. Leave local maps, too.

473 maps

Depending on the number of maps you have, categorize them first by region and then put them in alphabetical order. Shoe boxes hold them nicely. Label the boxes clearly, and remember that maps often become dated after a few years.

474 travel arrangements

Keep a file labeled "travel arrangements." In the file, make note of car rental, hotel, and airline phone numbers, with notes about companies you particularly like or don't like and include special discount coupons you may want to use. Also keep a list of standing arrangements, questions to ask, and special requests you will want to make whenever you make travel arrangements. These things may include special diets on a plane or a certain seat, a note to remember to use your frequent flyer numbers when you make reservations or to ask for a double bed, no-smoking accommodations, or whether the hotel has a gym. List those things that always come up but that you sometimes forget.

475 AAA

The Automobile Association of America has great maps for car travel, and they're free to members. They will also create a Trip-Tik for you that lays out your trip on maps, but not unless you ask them to. Don't forget to take advantage of the clubs you belong to. If you belong to AAA, remember to ask at hotels if they give a discount to AAA members. Keep a list of available discounts in your travel file. Take it out whenever you make travel arrangements.

476 before you go

Keep a list of things to do before traveling such as stopping the newspaper, putting the lights on timers, or asking someone to take care of your pet, water your plants, or take in the mail. If you always use the same luggage, keep the list in your luggage along with your list of things to pack. Otherwise, keep both lists in your "travel arrangements" file.

477 when I'm away

Make a list to keep on hand for people who look after your home when you're away. The list should include phone numbers for the plumber and electrician, the name and number of a person to call in an emergency, what to do in a variety of emergencies, the plant-watering or dog-feeding schedule, instructions for forwarding the mail, and so on. Attach a separate page with last-minute details and your current itinerary, including phone numbers where you can be reached.

478 picture yourself

When making a list of what to buy or what to pack, imagine yourself on your trip. Visualize your travel. Picture yourself waking up. What will be the first thing you'll need? Before lunch? When you leave the hotel? What will you be wearing? Carrying? Seeing? If you take the time to do this, chances are you'll have everything you need—no more and no less—and that should be your goal.

479 keep it packed

Keep your suitcase packed with an adapter for overseas travel; a travel hair dryer; a travel alarm clock; a cosmetics bag; and a checklist for remembering your comb, Swiss army knife, toothbrush, contact lens solutions, and other last-minute toiletries. If you travel frequently, buy a really light cotton robe, and keep it packed in your suitcase, too. You won't believe how handy such an item can be.

480 on trial

Trial-sized products are great for travel, but don't keep packing and unpacking them. Leave your suitcase packed with products you use when you travel: a pint-sized shampoo, shaving cream, a razor, toothpaste, powder, hand cream, and so on. It's a good idea to keep these items in a plastic toiletry organizer so they pack compactly without spilling and can be carried all together to a hotel or motel bathroom. Plastic see-through toiletry organizers that fold up into small packages are especially efficient. The best ones fold open and can be hung on a hook in a bathroom.

481 toiletries

Try to pack exactly the amount you're going to use of each disposable item. Trial sizes are of no value to you if they run out, leaving you to go out in search of shampoo, aspirin, or contact lens solution. Your goal should be to pack just enough so that you will use up each disposable item on your last day away and make room in your suitcase for any new purchases.

482 clothes for travel

Wardrobe planning is very important when you travel. Try to see that everything goes with everything. Plan your wardrobe around one or two colors so you can pack less. Black and white are generally good choices because they go with all other colors and are appropriate during the day and at night. Black is better in colder months, and white is better in the summer and in tropical climates. If you like, introduce a third color as an accent.

483 think square

Square things are easier to pack than round things. Choose square-shaped toiletries. Put non-square things in square boxes, and totally fill the boxes. The boxes will pack better than the individual items. Pack square things next to each other, and stack them.

484 neat and clean

Don't leave space when you pack. Put socks in shoes. Clothes are less likely to rumple if you put shoes and other heavy items on the bottom. Wrap shoes in plastic to make sure the bottoms don't touch clean clothing. Pack an extra plastic bag for bringing home dirty laundry.

485 pack for the plane

Why not consider the flight as part of the trip and enjoy it? Pack a bag just for the plane. Include thick, comfortable cotton socks. Take off your shoes the moment you get on board and slip into these. Bring bottled water so that you're not at the mercy of the flight attendants (you should drink lots of water when you're on a plane). Bring a couple of pieces of fruit or another snack that you like so you can eat on your own schedule. If it will make you more comfortable (or to make it clear to the person next to you that you're not interested in chattering), bring foam earplugs and sunglasses or a headset. Pack you own book or magazine so you won't have to worry about what's available on the plane.

486 quick change

The day before you leave, make sure you've got change for phones and dollars for tips. Break a twenty-dollar bill into eighteen ones and eight quarters. If you forget to do this before you leave, you should do it as soon as you arrive at your destination.

487 one bag

If you don't have to check your luggage when you fly, don't. If you can manage to fit everything into one bag that goes under your seat and, perhaps, a garment bag, do it. Take your luggage with you on the plane. You won't risk losing your belongings and you won't have to waste time at the other end waiting for them.

488 nothing counted, everything lost

Before you leave on a trip, count the number of parcels, bags, or pieces of luggage you have. Include your coat if there's a chance you will take it off, and your camera it it's not in a larger bag. Whenever you put things down and pick them up, count everything again before moving on. Do this every time you stop and start until you arrive at your destination.

489 taxi trick

In a taxi (or on a city bus), don't put anything down. Wrap whatever you can around your arm, such as the straps from all pocketbooks, shopping bags, and umbrellas, and keep the rest on your lap. If it's on your lap or wrapped around you, you're less likely to leave it on the seat or the floor.

490 arriving

Soon after you arrive at a hotel, orient yourself. Locate the local convenience store, drugstore, dry cleaner, hairdresser, and, if you intend to use it, the hotel mailroom. Ask at the concierge desk right away for a good local map, specific recommendations, and directions to the places you plan to visit the same day. If you arrive in the afternoon and are going out in the evening, ask for an iron or request any other services well in advance.

491 when I get back

In the last few days before you leave on a trip, start a list of things you need to do when you get back at home and at work, such as phone calls to make, repairs to take care of, and letters to write. List things that can wait, but that you don't want to forget or be plagued with remembering while you're gone. When you get back, you won't have to reconstruct your whole life.

492 temporary travel notebook

When you travel, don't take your whole year's appointment calendar with you unless you need it. Take a temporary travel notebook, instead. In it record your name, itinerary, and numbers of places you'll be in case you lose it on your trip. List names and addresses of people to write, send gifts to, or look up. Staple a half pocket in back for stamps, receipts, postcards, and other loose items. If you already use a personal organizer such as Day Runner, Filofax, or Day-Timer, it can be pared down and enhanced just for this purpose.

493 mini-mess

When you're packing to go home, if you're tempted to take the shampoo, body lotion, conditioner, shoe shine kit, sewing kit, and deodorant soap, think again. You didn't even use them because you prefer your own brands. Remember your bathroom at home where a hundred such miniamenities are gathering dust. When you get back, get rid of them; give them to a friend who uses them, or throw them away if they're old.

494 oh, no!

You bought too much on your trip and it doesn't all fit in your suitcase, or it's too heavy to drag to the airport by yourself. Don't panic. If you're at a hotel, see if they have a shipping department. If they do, get a box and mail home all the items you won't need right away. Or go to a post office and do the same thing.

495 extra business cards

If you travel on business, leave some extra business cards packed in your suitcase—just in case.

496 mail bag

If you plan to mail things home, like catalogs from a convention, or if you plan to acquire items that you feel comfortable mailing, take your own packing materials. Line your suitcase with jiffy bags. Include mailing tape, postage, and a scissors. Most hotels will ship packages UPS, Federal Express or express mail, or first class (you may want to find out ahead of time whether the hotel you're going to has this service). If you mail your packages a few days before you return home yourself, you may find them waiting for you.

497 expense envelope

Bring an envelope with you for keeping business receipts, and put the receipts in it as soon as you get them. Try to remember to make a notation in your expense book at the same time. A little work now will be worth a lot to you later.

498 expense money

When you're traveling for business, before you leave your house count your money so that you'll know to account for it. If you take your own money—as you should—make sure you keep it in a separate compartment or wallet.

499 credit is best

When you travel on business, it is advisable to charge as much as possible and minimize cash expenses. For every cash expense, you need to request a receipt and make a notation and you risk forgetting. Your credit card charges will show up on your monthly statement whether you've made a note in your expense book or not.

500 that's B.O.S.S.

It's important to keep track of your expenses when you travel on business. Notations can be made on a microcassette recorder, in a notebook, in an expense book, or on the back of a match cover, but if you use a computer and travel on business often, the best way to keep track of business expenses is with an electronic organizer such as Expense Easy Plus, which can be adapted to Casio's Executive B.O.S.S. hand-held computer. You punch in the expense, and the computer logs, adds, sorts, and distributes it. It does even more, but what more could you want?

INDEX